T0275717

# Structured Search for Big Data
## From Keywords to Key-objects

# Structured Search for Big Data
## From Keywords to Key-objects

Mikhail Gilula

ELSEVIER

AMSTERDAM • BOSTON • HEIDELBERG
LONDON • NEW YORK • OXFORD
PARIS • SAN DIEGO • SAN FRANCISCO
SINGAPORE • SYDNEY • TOKYO

Morgan Kaufmann is an imprint of Elsevier

Morgan Kaufmann is an imprint of Elsevier
225 Wyman Street, Waltham, MA 02451, USA

Copyright © 2016 Elsevier Inc. All rights reserved.

No part of this publication may be reproduced or transmitted in any form or by any means, electronic or mechanical, including photocopying, recording, or any information storage and retrieval system, without permission in writing from the publisher. Details on how to seek permission, further information about the Publisher's permissions policies and our arrangements with organizations such as the Copyright Clearance Center and the Copyright Licensing Agency, can be found at our website: www.elsevier.com/permissions.

This book and the individual contributions contained in it are protected under copyright by the Publisher (other than as may be noted herein).

**Notices**
Knowledge and best practice in this field are constantly changing. As new research and experience broaden our understanding, changes in research methods, professional practices, or medical treatment may become necessary.

Practitioners and researchers must always rely on their own experience and knowledge in evaluating and using any information, methods, compounds, or experiments described herein. In using such information or methods they should be mindful of their own safety and the safety of others, including parties for whom they have a professional responsibility.

To the fullest extent of the law, neither the Publisher nor the authors, contributors, or editors, assume any liability for any injury and/or damage to persons or property as a matter of products liability, negligence or otherwise, or from any use or operation of any methods, products, instructions, or ideas contained in the material herein.

ISBN: 978-0-12-804631-9

**British Library Cataloguing-in-Publication Data**
A catalogue record for this book is available from the British Library

**Library of Congress Cataloging-in-Publication Data**
A catalog record for this book is available from the Library of Congress

For information on all Morgan Kaufmann publications
visit our website at www.mkp.com

Working together
to grow libraries in
developing countries

www.elsevier.com • www.bookaid.org

# Dedication

*To my parents, Max and Asya; my wife, Natalia; my children, Maria, Victoria, and Maxim; and my grandson, Sava.*

# CONTENTS

# QUOTATION

*Getting information off the Internet is like taking a drink from a fire hydrant.*
Mitchell Kapor

## OBJECTIVE

We are now in the Big Data era, which is characterized by three Vs: Volume, Variety, and Velocity. This new VVV world not surprisingly follows the WWW one.

While large data volumes are not uncommon for traditional databases, it is mostly the other two Vs that spell trouble. When data structures vary or change rapidly, the classic database technology becomes not as useful. At the same time, NoSQL share is growing, though some say these are not even databases because they generally do not aim to support ad hoc queries or full-blown query languages. Proponents of NoSQL point out that ad hoc querying is not necessary for many applications, but rich data structures and high availability along with speed of access are paramount. High availability may not be a decisive differentiator, but the rich data structure handling and ease of access to data from applications do not belong to the advantages of SQL databases. It is worth mentioning that some data from NoSQL databases end up in SQL data warehouses for analytical processing.

Another big trend of the WWW–VVV era is the ubiquitous use of keyword search. Internet search companies have immensely advanced the technology and that probably accounts for use cases where the keyword search alone is a suboptimal solution. One example is e-commerce where goods and services are searched by keywords rather than by specifications, which would be the case in the database paradigm of structured queries. If the structured query interfaces were used, researching complex merchandise for the best deals would take minutes instead of hours it might take with keywords. A typical remedy is classifiers helping users reduce search outputs by checking the classification boxes. It requires classifying each item individually but falls short of providing the on par functionality. This is essentially equivalent to labeling the table rows with multiple tags in lieu of employing query languages.

The above suggests that we may be failing to uncover Big Information by not fully interrogating Big Data with structured queries. The question is do we want to, or are we fine with just keywords and NoSQL.

Our goal is to present the advantages of structured search in the realm of Big Data so that the readers will be better informed to answer this question.

## AUDIENCE

This book is for a wide audience of enlightened readers defined by the dictionary as "factually well-informed, tolerant of alternative opinions, and guided by rational thought." It is addressed to anyone who works with, studies, or simply is interested in Big Data, SQL or NoSQL databases, information retrieval, or Internet search. This includes, but is not limited to, IT professionals and managers, data architects and modelers, software developers, undergraduate and graduate students in information systems, computer science or engineering, and their teachers as well. Some parts can be useful for business professionals, students and teachers, especially for those working or planning to work in e-commerce.

The book does not require special training in computer science or programming skills. An introductory course in information systems or databases should suffice for understanding most of the material. We have tried to make it brief, interesting, and thought provoking.

## OUTLINE OF THE BOOK

Chapter 1 conceptualizes structured search as a technology for querying multiple data sources in an independent and scalable manner. It occupies the middle ground between keyword search and database search. As in the keyword search paradigm, query originators do not need to know the structure or the number of data sources being queried. As in the database paradigm, users can pose precise queries, control the output order, and access data in real time.

Chapter 2 introduces key-objects as a generalization of keywords. The key-objects can be thought of as data structures reflecting the properties or characteristics of things and re-encapsulating them from their names presented by keywords. For example, the keyword "chair" does not allow distinguishing between different chairs; and therefore, does not allow narrowing the search down to specific chair instances. A key-object "chair" allows specification of the chair properties the query originators may be looking for, and there is no limit to the number of different key-objects reflecting the concept of a chair. Keywords allow posing queries independently of the indexed documents or web pages, that is, without knowledge of their content, or number. Similarly, key-objects allow posing queries to structured data sources without knowledge of their organization or the number of data sources being queried.

The key-object concept is further developed in Chapter 3. It presents an abstract key-object data model based on hereditarily-finite sets – a mathematical structure having the finite set as the only constructor. The key-object model is a generalization of the relational model where data objects – key-object instances – can be arbitrarily structured and multi-valued, and the phenomenon of multiple values receives its formal explication. Sets of key-object instances form data stores, which can be viewed as analogs of relational tables and databases at the same time. Particularly, tables correspond to flat homogeneous data stores and databases correspond to flat data stores.

All relational operations have their generalized analogs in data store operations of the key-object model. Unlike their relational counterparts, all operations on data stores are total, that is, defined for any operands, whereas relational set-theoretic operations, for example, are only defined for relations having an equal number of attributes of compatible types. The totality of data store operations contributes to scalability of the native data store systems because any two data stores can be viewed as the parts of one and the same data store. In the relational setting that would correspond to any two tables being the parts of one and the same table. Under this analogy, the same query could be addressed to all tables in all databases and the response could be formed as the union of responses returned from each table.

Chapter 4 introduces design principles, framework, and data architecture for structured search systems based on the key-object model. It presents eight design principles of the systems realizing the structured search paradigm. They include query independence, search scalability, security control, and others. Not all principles may be important or useful for all cases. However, the presented framework and data architecture aim to satisfy all listed principles so that the designers of concrete systems could choose a mix of features they need to implement.

The functions of the systems are as follows: facilitating query origination, delivering queries to data providers, collecting responses to the queries from the data providers, and delivering the responses to the query originators. Key-object catalogs provide federating namespaces for the structured search systems. Queries are explicated using the KeySQL language and are delivered to data providers using the Q-format. Responses are returned using the R-format designed for transporting key-object instances. Those formats can be machine and user readable or binary for increased performance.

Two principle types of structured search systems are considered: federative and native. In the federative scenario, data manipulation is limited to the federative SELECT statement. In a sense, this mimics the keyword search where no inserts, updates, or deletes can be performed. In the native scenario, the full data manipulation functionality is available.

Chapter 5 describes KeySQL – a structured query language based on the key-object data model. It consists of two main parts: catalog management language (CML) and store manipulation language (SML), and provides two types of data manipulation functionality via the federative and native sublanguages. The sublanguages share the major part of CML, but have no SML statements in common. CML plays the role of data definition language and deals with creating and dropping key-objects, catalogs, and synonymies. The federative SML includes only the federative SELECT statement. The native SML includes CREATE, DROP, INSERT, SELECT, UPDATE, and DELETE statements for the data stores as sets of key-object instances.

The positioning of structured search within the landscape of historical and contemporary database trends is discussed in Chapter 6. The topics considered are: key-objects and object-oriented programming paradigm, key-objects and object-oriented databases, KeySQL and NoSQL, query independence and data independence, and KeySQL and MPP architectures.

Chapter 7 presents examples of structured search solutions, applications, and use cases. They include e-commerce and mobile e-commerce applications, secure federated information systems, healthcare information systems, Big Data warehousing, implementation of KeySQL on MapReduce clusters, and others.

The last section is devoted to the place of structured search in the Internet evolution. It describes an implementation of structured Internet search via key-object instances linked or embedded into web pages. The key-object instances are then collected by search engines, stored, and made available for the structured search. Alternatively, a real-time structured Internet search can be employed. In this setting, websites become data providers and play an active role in the search instead of waiting for search engines to collect their data. Real-time and nonreal-time search results can be combined within the federative framework.

## US PATENTS

The book comprises material protected by granted and pending US patents.

# ACKNOWLEDGMENTS

Konstantin Andreyev was one of the first to recognize the potential of structured search; with the help of Alex Kouznetsov, he created the first structured search portal and worked with Alexander Denisov on the implementation of KeySQL catalog management.

ZEDventures and personally Saurbh Khera organized a series of presentations, which helped shaping the book.

Maxim Gilula read through several versions of the text and helped to clean it up.

The value of constructive critical remarks made by Alexei Lisitsa, Alexei Stolboushkin, Seva Yakhontov, and Vladas Leonas cannot be overestimated.

Chris Date, Paul Smoot, and Shell Finkelstein have encouraged me over the years.

I am very grateful to all these people, and also to everyone who took the time to participate in the structured search presentations.

**Mikhail Gilula**
Foster City, CA, 2015

# CHAPTER 1

# Introduction to Structured Search

*It is contrary to reason to say that there is a vacuum or space in which there is absolutely nothing.*

**Rene Descartes (Principia Philosophiae, 1644)**

## 1.1 LIMITATIONS OF KEYWORD SEARCH

Contemporary search engines operate within the information retrieval (IR) paradigm where the search criteria consist of keywords and the search results are lists of web pages or, generally, lists of documents (texts), which include the specified combinations of keywords.

IR existed in different forms long before the introduction of computers and its limitations motivated the query concept research resulting in database languages like SQL. For example, in 1960s and 1970s it was popular to talk about the "factographic" systems, which would enable searching for information or facts *per se* as opposed to searching for documents, such as books, patents, or articles, that may or may not contain the relevant information. The new IR incarnation came with the Internet and was advanced by the Internet search providers.

The main limitations of the keyword search are as follows.

*Intrinsic search imprecision.* By using only keywords, it is generally difficult to determine the real question existing in the mind of the query originator because the same keywords may be used to pose different questions. Also, when trying to narrow down the search by adding more keywords, there is a greater risk of not finding the relevant information.

*Search results only for humans.* Since the results of the keyword search are typically the documents conveying information in natural languages, it is not easy to process the search results programmatically – not involving the human recipient. Of course, the web pages are always somewhat structured and sometimes consist of quite structured information, but the structure of each individual page is not known *a priori* and the difficulties of processing natural languages programmatically always remain.

*No user control over output order.* The ordering of search results is controlled by search engines and is a valuable trade secret. Some e-commerce websites allow users to sort search results by the price of merchandise. However, since the results are produced using keywords, the users often need to look through most of the returned items anyway. For example, currently when a user of a big Internet marketplace specifies a model of a digital camera to search for, and chooses the "Price: lowest first" option, the first couple of hundred items in the output are not the listings of the camera but instead are the camera accessories because they tend to be cheaper.

*No security control.* To index a document or a web page, search engines need full access to the source. In this context, security of information or parts of information has no place or meaning.

*No real-time access.* Processing web pages and updating indexes takes time. It could be days or weeks before the updated web pages would appear in search results. Information can become stale or completely disappear during this period.

*Search engines are not green.* Due to keyword search imprecision, most information returned by search engines is never viewed or consumed by users. This means excessive CPU and IO cycles, network traffic, and watts of energy are wasted in data centers.

## 1.2 KEYWORD SEARCH IN E-COMMERCE

One of the areas underserved by the keyword search is e-commerce. For example, there is no general way to search for all digital cameras with optical zoom more than 10, more than 10 megapixels, weighing less than 10 oz, and so on. The basic problems of locating merchandise using the keyword search are as follows.

*Inability of finding merchandise directly by specifications rather than by keywords like brand or model needed to retrieve product specifications.* Research of complex items may take hours and still does not guarantee the best deals. It would be vastly more efficient to search by multiple item characteristics at once instead of going back and forth through dozens or hundreds of descriptions in order to compare them by several parameters.

*The search output rankings are generally unrelated to the qualities of merchandise (i.e., specifications) or the deals offered.* Since the search results tend to be voluminous, high search ranks are critical for merchants. The keyword search puts buyers at a disadvantage because they are only able to look through the first few pages of an output, and whereby a better deal may be on the next page that they did not get to.

To alleviate these problems, e-merchants use the following main techniques.

- Improving product search rankings by implementing a variety of learning algorithms aimed at extracting more information from the natural language search inputs, in particular by analyzing the shopping behavior of the users.
- Classifying the merchandise into search categories to minimize search outputs.

However these techniques bring difficulties of their own and do not avoid the aforementioned problems altogether. Particularly, the classifiers require individual processing of each item description to assign it to the classifier categories that vary from store to store. If the categories change, the items need to be reprocessed. The classifiers are fixed and work only via an equality predicate. It is generally difficult to negate a feature, for example, saying one needs a printer with no duplex mode, or to specify one of an infinite number of conditions, which are not a part of the classifier at hand.

As a result, millions and millions of hours are spent annually by customers trying to locate the right merchandise or services, and to research and compare them in order to receive the best deals. Another problem is the time it takes to sort through the voluminous responses generated by a keyword search.

## 1.3 LIMITATIONS OF DATABASE SEARCH

The traditional alternative to the IR is the database paradigm, where the search criteria are formulated using a rich set of predicates and are evaluated on collections of structured records comprising typed fields, like numeric or character ones. Results of the database search are always precise, can be ordered by users, and can be programmatically processed since the semantics of each field is known *a priori*.

However, unlike the keyword search it is not that easy to query a database. The query originator needs to know table names, column names, possibly units of measurement used in the tables, codes for certain values, etc.

The search scalability problems arise when multiple databases or structured stores need to be accessed and the search results need to be combined. In the database world, adding data sources is much more complex than in the world of keyword search, where it is completely transparent; probably thousands of new data sources – web pages – participate in the Internet searches every day.

Table 1.1 illustrates relative advantages and limitations of the two traditional query paradigms.

| Table 1.1  Keyword Search Versus Database Search | | |
|---|---|---|
| Features | Keyword Search | Database Search |
| Queries are independent from data sources | Yes | No |
| Search is scalable – new data sources easily added | Yes | No |
| Search precision not affected by scale | No | Yes |
| Search output not only for humans | No | Yes |
| Users can control output order | No | Yes |
| Security control | No | Yes |
| Real-time access | No | Yes |

## 1.4  WHAT IS STRUCTURED SEARCH?

Structured search is a technology for querying multiple data sources in independent and scalable manner. It occupies the middle ground between keyword search and database search. As in the keyword search paradigm, query originators need not know the structure or the number of data sources being queried. As in the database paradigm, users can formulate precise structured queries, control the output order, and access information in real time.

The goal is to achieve the best of both worlds as shown in Table 1.2.

| Table 1.2 Structured Search Versus Keyword Search and Database Search | | | |
|---|---|---|---|
| Features | Keyword Search | Database Search | Structured Search |
| Queries are independent from data sources | Yes | No | Yes |
| Search is scalable – new data sources easily added | Yes | No | Yes |
| Search precision is not affected by scale | No | Yes | Yes |
| Search output is not only for humans | No | Yes | Yes |
| Users can control output order | No | Yes | Yes |
| Information security | No | Yes | Yes |
| Real-time access | No | Yes | Yes |

# CHAPTER 2

# Key-Objects vs. Keywords

*I have mislaid the key. I sniff the spray*
*And think of nothing; I see and hear nothing;*

**Edward Thomas (Old Man)**

## 2.1 INTRODUCING KEY-OBJECTS

The structured search paradigm based on key-objects proceeds from analogy between the structured search and the keyword search where key-objects play the role of keywords, hence the name. As we know, keywords allow posing queries independently of indexed documents or web pages, that is, without knowledge of their organization, content, or number. Similarly, key-objects allow posing queries to structured data sources without knowledge of their logical organization or the number of data sources being queried.

The key-objects can be thought of as data structures reflecting properties or characteristics of things and re-encapsulating them from their names presented by keywords. For example, the keyword "chair" does not allow distinguishing between different chairs; and therefore, does not allow narrowing the search down to specific chair instances. A key-object "chair" allows specification of the chair properties the query originators may be looking for, and there is no limit to the number of different key-objects reflecting the concept of a chair in their own way.

The key-object data model is founded in a mathematical structure of hereditarily-finite sets. It is arguably the simplest structure with only one constructor that can naturally incorporate both relational and non-relational data, like those used in XML or JSON. However, conversely to XML and JSON, it is an abstract data model with set operations, like the relational one but more capacious and flexible. The key-object data model is described in Chapter 3. This chapter provides an informal introduction to key-objects.

In the framework of structured search, the relations like synonymy, analogous to the paradigmatic relations between keywords, can be specified on key-objects. The relations enable a structured query expansion analogous to the query expansion in information retrieval.

## 2.2 MARY'S PRINTER

Mary needs a simple monochrome laser printer and she does not want to pay for the duplex mode capability; altogether the specifications appear as in Figure 2.1.

1. Printing method: laser
2. No duplex mode
3. Horizontal resolution: at least 600 dpi
4. Vertical resolution: at least 600 dpi
5. Speed of printing: at least 14 ppm

*Fig. 2.1. Mary's printer specifications.*

It is not easy to find it using a search engine. The search engines are not good at numbers or negations. There is no problem finding specifications by the brand and model keywords, but it is not easy to find brands and models by the desired specifications.

## 2.3 KEY-OBJECTS AND INSTANCES

To be able to formulate queries about goods, services, and other things, we need to conceptualize or virtualize them in some way. For example, to formulate queries about printers, we need the concept of a printer and the more detailed queries we need to formulate, the more detailed printer concept we need. In this section, we introduce *key-objects* as a means of virtualizing things in order to formulate structured queries.

### 2.3.1 Key-Objects

Key-objects either consist of other (smaller) key-objects or are *atomic*. Each atomic key-object has a *type*.

For example, Figure 2.2 shows a non-atomic key-object PRINTER_B, which is supposed to mean a monochrome (black and white) printer.

```
PRINTER_B {DUPLEX_MODE,
           MANUFACTURER,
           MODEL,
           PRICE,
           PRINT_RESOLUTION,
           PRINT_SPEED_B_PPM,
           PRINTING_METHOD},
DUPLEX_MODE number,
MANUFACTURER string,
MODEL string,
PRICE number,
PRINT_RESOLUTION {RESOLUTION_H_DPI,
                  RESOLUTION_V_DPI},
PRINT_SPEED_B_PPM number,
PRINTING_METHOD string
RESOLUTION_H_DPI number,
RESOLUTION_V_DPI number;
```

*Fig. 2.2. A printer key-object and key-objects it contains.*

It consists of six atomic key-objects, as follows,

```
DUPLEX_MODE,
MANUFACTURER,
MODEL,
PRICE,
PRINT_SPEED_B_PPM,
PRINTING_METHOD
```

and one nonatomic key-object,

```
PRINT_RESOLUTION
```

which in turn consists of two atomic key-objects.

```
RESOLUTION_H_DPI,
RESOLUTION_V_DPI.
```

The types of the atomic key-objects are shown next to them.

The names of key-objects are deemed case insensitive, and we use the upper and lower case names interchangeably. For example, PRINTER_B or printer_b.

Before finishing this section, let us return to the key-object definition to make it more precise. In order to do so, we use the mathematical notion of finite set meaning an unordered collection of unique elements. Basically, we point out that nonatomic key-objects are finite sets of key-objects they consist of.

## 2.3.2 Key-Object Instances

An *instance of an atomic key-object* is an ordered pair <object, value>, where the value either belongs to the object type or is *NULL*, which means it is unknown.

To present the instances of atomic key-objects we use the notation *object: value*, as in the following example (Figure 2.3).

```
DUPLEX_MODE:0
```

*Fig. 2.3.  Instance of atomic key-object.*

A nonatomic key-object becomes an *instance of the nonatomic key-object* when each key-object it comprises, is replaced by an instance of the key-object, as in the following example (Figure 2.4).

```
PRINTER_B:  {DUPLEX_MODE:0,
             MANUFACTURER:NULL,
             MODEL:'A1',
             PRICE:99.99,
             PRINT_RESOLUTION:{RESOLUTION_H_DPI:600,
                               RESOLUTION_V_DPI:600},
             PRINT_SPEED_B_PPM:14,
             PRINTING_METHOD:'LASER'}
```

*Fig. 2.4.  Instance of nonatomic key-object.*

While key-objects represent concepts of things, key-object instances represent instances of things. For example, search results are key-object instances satisfying the search criteria.

*Note*: Generally, the multivalued instances can be considered, and we will return to this topic in Chapter 3.

## 2.4 CATALOGS AND QUERY EXPANSION

### 2.4.1 Querying via Key-Objects

To be able to relate to a particular key-object and to use it for querying, we assume that all key-objects currently available are included in a *key-object catalog*.

Figure 2.5 shows how the monochrome printer key-object can be used to formulate Mary's query.

```
SELECT printer_b
OF CATALOG MyCatalog
WHERE duplex_mode = 0
    AND resolution_h_dpi >= 600
    AND resolution_v_dpi >= 600
    AND print_speed_b_ppm >= 14
    AND printing_method = 'LASER'
ORDER BY price ASC;
```

*Fig. 2.5. Mary's query using key-object* PRINTER_B.

It looks like an SQL query with the "from" clause replaced by the "of catalog" clause. In terms of key-objects, the query means: *return all instances of* PRINTER_B *key-object of catalog* MyCatalog *with combinations of values of comprising atomic key-object instances conforming to the "where" clause, and sort them by values of the* PRICE *instances in ascending order.*

### 2.4.2 More Query Examples

In the previous section, we saw an example of a query that looks like an SQL query without the "from" clause. However, this resemblance may be misleading due to several differences. One of them can be illustrated by rewriting the query as in Figure 2.6.

Here, atomic key-objects RESOLUTION_H_DPI and RESOLUTION_V_DPI are qualified by key-object PRINT_RESOLUTION they immediately belong to.

The reason is that several atomic key-objects residing on different levels within a key-object specified in the "select" clause may happen

```
SELECT printer_b
OF CATALOG MyCatalog
WHERE duplex_mode = 0
   AND print_resolution.resolution_h_dpi >= 600
   AND print_resolution.resolution_v_dpi >= 600
   AND print_speed_b_ppm >= 14
   AND printing_method = 'LASER'
ORDER BY price ASC;
```

*Fig. 2.6.  General form of Mary's query.*

to be the same, and we may need to distinguish between them. Generally, the qualification may span more than one level. However, the initial and simpler looking query is accurate since it can be uniquely interpreted.

This reminds us that while SQL deals with "flat" tables, the structure of key-objects is hierarchical. However, a more profound difference between the key-object query paradigm and the relational one lies in another plane.

A result of any SQL query is always a single table with a set of columns defined by the query. In the key-object world, the reply may comprise instances of several different key-objects and those may not be predetermined by the query alone. This feature reflects the basic idea of query independence for the structured queries and is in a sense analogous to the query independence of the keyword search.

Consider the following query (Figure 2.7).

```
SELECT *
OF CATALOG MyCatalog
WHERE last_name = 'Moriarty';
```

*Fig. 2.7.  Query having no SQL analogs.*

In the key-object world, the asterisk in the "select" clause means "any key-object of MyCatalog catalog." And the query means: get all instances of all key-objects containing at any level an instance of atomic key-object LAST_NAME with the value 'Moriarty'.

Another query is given in Figure 2.8.

```
SELECT *
OF CATALOG MyCatalog
WHERE last_name = *;
```

*Fig. 2.8. Another query (not in SQL).*

This query is supposed to return all instances of all key-objects containing any instance of atomic key-object LAST_NAME at any level. In fact the asterisk in the "where" clause is a shorthand notation, and the query in the full form is as follows.

```
SELECT *
OF CATALOG MyCatalog
WHERE last_name IS NULL
    OR last_name IS NOT NULL;
```

Of course, each of the two previously mentioned queries can be expanded or rewritten into a set of queries, each of which has only one key-object in the "select" clause. This is done by picking all key-objects from MyCatalog catalog that include key-object LAST_NAME at any level and addressing the query to each key-object individually.

Query results in the previous examples may include instances of several key-objects because the "select" clause explicitly permits that. However, the same may happen even when the "select" clause specifies a single key-object but the query is *expanded* using the catalog.

### 2.4.3 Catalogs With Relations
The *relations,* particularly the *synonymy* relations, may be defined on the key-objects. As we shall see in Section 2.4.4, catalogs comprising relations enable more sophisticated query expansion techniques than the one illustrated in Section 2.4.2.

Here, we create a sample catalog to work with.

Figure 2.9 shows an exemplary fragment of a key-object catalog.

```
BRAND string =  [ MANUFACTURER ]  ,
COPIER_B {...} ,
COPIER_C {...} ,
DUPLEX_MODE  number ,
FAX_MACHINE_B {...} ,
FAX_MACHINE_C {...} ,
MANUFACTURER string  = [ BRAND ]  ,
MODEL string ,
MULTIFUNCTION_B {BRAND ,
                COPIER_B ,
                FAX_MACHINE_B ,
                MODEL ,
                PRICE ,
                PRINTER_B ,
                SCANNER_B} ,
MULTIFUNCTION_C {BRAND ,
                COPIER_C ,
                FAX_MACHINE_C ,
                MODEL ,
                PRICE ,
                PRINTER_ C,
                SCANNER_ C} ,
PRICE number ,
PRINT_RESOLUTION  {RESOLUTION_H_DPI ,
                   RESOLUTION_V_DPI },
PRINT_SPEED_B_PPM  number ,
PRINT_SPEED_C_PPM  number ,
PRINTER_B { DUPLEX_MODE ,
            MANUFACTURER ,
            MODEL ,
            PRICE ,
            PRINT_RESOLUTION ,
            PRINT_SPEED_B_PPM ,
            PRINTING_METHOD} ,
PRINTER_C {BRAND ,
            DUPLEX_MODE ,
            MODEL ,
            PRICE ,
            PRINT_RESOLUTION ,
            PRINT_SPEED_B_PPM ,
            PRINT_SPEED_C_PPM ,
            PRINTING_METHOD} ,
PRINTING_METHOD string ,
RESOLUTION_H_DPI  number,
RESOLUTION_V_DPI  number,
SCANNER_B {...};
```

*Fig. 2.9. Key-object catalog example.*

The catalog includes the following atomic key-objects:

```
BRAND,
DUPLEX_MODE,
MANUFACTURER,
MODEL,
PRICE,
PRINT_SPEED_B_PPM,
PRINT_SPEED_C_PPM,
PRINTING_METHOD
RESOLUTION_H_DPI,
RESOLUTION_V_DPI,
```

Key-objects, BRAND and MANUFACTURER are defined as *synonyms* by setting BRAND equal to MANUFACTURER and vice versa.

The catalog includes the following nonatomic key-objects:

```
COPIER_B,
COPIER_C,
FAX_MACHINE_B,
FAX_MACHINE_C,
MULTIFUNCTION_B,
MULTIFUNCTION_C,
PRINT_RESOLUTION,
PRINTER_B,
PRINTER_C,
SCANNER_B,
SCANNER_C
```

Except for PRINT_RESOLUTION, they exemplify different classes of printers, scanners, copiers, fax machines, and multifunction peripherals. The multifunction peripherals are the most complex things and comprise monochrome or color printers, scanners, copiers, and fax machines. The structure of the scanners, copiers, and fax machines is not shown in order to save space.

### 2.4.4 Query Expansion
Query expansion techniques are based on relations and structural compositions of key-objects defined in catalogs.

In this section, we present an example of a simple query expansion algorithm that uses a synonymy relation. The example is based on the catalog fragment from Section 2.4.3, which includes two synonyms: BRAND and MANUFACTURER.

Consider the following query (Figure 2.10).

```
SELECT printer_b
OF CATALOG MyCatalog
WHERE manufacturer IS NOT NULL
    AND duplex_mode = 0
    AND print_resolution.resolution_h_dpi >= 600
    AND print_resolution.resolution_v_dpi >= 600
    AND print_speed_b_ppm >= 14
    AND printing_method = 'laser'
EXPAND;
```

*Fig. 2.10. Original query for key-object* PRINTER_B.

Given this original query and the catalog, the expansion algorithm will produce a set of four queries listed in Figure 2.11 in the alphabetical order. The original query results are complemented with results of all queries produced by the expansion algorithm as follows:

1. Query #3 is directed to PRINTER_B key-object and is produced by default, independently of the "expand" option because it is the original query formulated by the user.
2. Query #4 is directed to PRINTER_C (a color printer) key-object because PRINTER_C contains all key-objects in the "where" clause of the original query, except MANUFACTURER. However, it contains the BRAND synonym for MANUFACTURER, as defined by the catalog. Thus, this query for PRINTER_C key-object is generated. The "where" clause of Query #4 is identical to the one of Query #3 except that MANUFACTURER is replaced by BRAND.
3. Query #1 is directed to MULTIFUNCTION_B key-object because it contains PRINTER_B key-object as defined by the catalog.
4. Finally, Query #2 is directed to MULTIFUNCTION_C key-object because MULTIFUNCTION_C contains PRINTER_C key-object as defined by the catalog. Since MULTIFUNCTION_C contains two occurrences of BRAND key-object, the target occurrence is qualified by the name of PRINTER_C key-object.

Though the query was originally formulated using a monochrome printer key-object, the expanded search may return not only the instances

```
                  /********** Query #1 **********/
SELECT multifunction_b
OF CATALOG MyCatalog
WHERE manufacturer IS NOT NULL
  AND duplex_mode = 0
  AND resolution_h_dpi >= 600
  AND resolution_v_dpi >= 600
  AND print_speed_b_ppm >= 14
  AND printing_method = 'laser';
                  /********** Query #2 **********/
SELECT multifunction_c
OF CATALOG MyCatalog
WHERE printer_c.brand IS NOT NULL
  AND duplex_mode = 0
  AND resolution_h_dpi >= 600
  AND resolution_v_dpi >= 600
  AND print_speed_b_ppm >= 14
  AND printing_method = 'laser';
                  /********** Query #3 **********/
SELECT printer_b
OF CATALOG MyCatalog
WHERE manufacturer IS NOT NULL
  AND duplex_mode = 0
  AND resolution_h_dpi >= 600
  AND resolution_v_dpi >= 600
  AND print_speed_b_ppm >= 14
  AND printing_method = 'laser'
                  /********** Query #4 **********/
SELECT printer_c
OF CATALOG MyCatalog
WHERE brand IS NOT NULL
  AND duplex_mode = 0
  AND resolution_h_dpi >= 600
  AND resolution_v_dpi >= 600
  AND print_speed_b_ppm >= 14
  AND printing_method = 'laser';
```

*Fig. 2.11. Query expansion output.*

of monochrome printers, but also color printers and monochrome or color multifunction peripherals. And that is because all of them may satisfy search criteria – use the laser method of printing, not have the duplex mode, print in black with the required speed and resolution, and have a manufacturer or a brand specified.

Let us note that there can be multiple algorithms of query expansion, which can be chosen for specific types of search. Our goal is to introduce the concept of query expansion for structured queries.

# CHAPTER 3

# Key-Object Data Model

*Today's scientists have substituted mathematics for experiments, and they wander off through equation, and eventually build a structure which has no relation to reality.*

Nicolas Tesla

*Model – shmodel...*

Unknown

## 3.1 KEY-OBJECTS AS HEREDITARILY-FINITE SETS

The mathematical structure of key-objects is the structure of hereditarily-finite sets constructed from atomic key-objects.

Atomic key-objects are represented by symbol sequences, or *words*, in some alphabet – particularly the words used to name them. This makes sense because each atomic key-object has only one type and we can think that the types are integrated into the names of atomic key-objects. If we consider only the words not containing a certain symbol, for example, colon ":", we could use two-part words <name>:<type> to represent atomic key-objects. But we use just the names for simplicity.

All nonatomic key-objects are sets. For example, PRINT_RESOLUTION corresponds to the set of two atomic key-objects as follows:

```
PRINT_RESOLUTION = {RESOLUTION_H_DPI, RESOLUTION_V_DPI}
```

The following is the set representing PRINTER_B key-object from our catalog:

```
{DUPLEX_MODE,
 MANUFACTURER,
 MODEL,
 PRICE,
 PRINT_RESOLUTION,
 PRINT_SPEED_B_PPM,
 PRINTING_METHOD}
```

## 3.2 OPERATIONS ON KEY-OBJECTS

### 3.2.1 Key-Object Naming

As mentioned, we name key-objects using the words in some alphabet and address key-objects by their names. However, key-objects produced from the named key-objects as the results of operations may not be named. Following the relational terminology, such key-objects are called *derived* key-objects as opposed to *base* key-objects, which are named key-objects of a catalog.

Derived key-objects can be left unnamed, but alternatively their names may be generated according to certain naming conventions. This can lead to situations when one and the same key-object can be referenced using more than one name. An example of such naming convention is introduced in succeeding sections with respect to the operation of composition.

Another case when more than one name may be used is when we need to distinguish between several occurrences of a key-object participating in an operation. The same operation of composition produces a relevant example.

Therefore, though a single name can be sufficient to address a key-object, philosophically, even atomic key-objects are not the same as their names. An analogous situation takes place in relational algebra, where a formal operation of renaming is sometimes introduced to deal with it. We leave the renaming at the intuitive level in order to simplify the presentation.

### 3.2.2 Union

The *union* of any two nonatomic key-objects is a key-object formed as the set-theoretic union of the sets corresponding to the operands. We use the plus sign "+" to denote the union.

For example, the union of PRINTER_B and PRINTER_C key-objects from our catalog of Section 2.4.3 is a derived key-object represented by the following set:

```
PRINTER_B + PRINTER_C = {BRAND,
                         DUPLEX_MODE,
                         MANUFACTURER,
                         MODEL,
                         PRICE,
                         PRINT_RESOLUTION,
                         PRINT_SPEED_B_PPM,
                         PRINT_SPEED_C_PPM,
                         PRINTING_METHOD}
```

### 3.2.3 Intersection

The *intersection* of any two nonatomic key-objects is a key-object formed as the set-theoretic intersection of the sets corresponding to the operands. We use the ampersand sign "&" to denote the intersection.

For example, the intersection of PRINTER_B and PRINTER_C key-objects from our catalog is a derived key-object represented by the following set:

```
PRINTER_B & PRINTER_C = {DUPLEX_MODE
                         MODEL,
                         PRICE,
                         PRINT_RESOLUTION,
                         PRINT_SPEED_B_PPM,
                         PRINTING_METHOD}
```

### 3.2.4 Difference

The *difference* of any two nonatomic key-objects is a key-object formed as the set-theoretic difference of the sets corresponding to the operands. We use the minus sign "-" to denote the difference.

For example, the difference of PRINTER_C and PRINTER_B key-objects from our catalog is a derived key-object represented by the following set:

```
PRINTER_C - PRINTER_B = {BRAND, PRINT_SPEED_C_PPM}
```

Unlike the union and intersection, the difference is not a commutative operation, for example, the difference of PRINTER_B and PRINTER_C is the following set:

```
PRINTER_B - PRINTER_C = {MANUFACTURER}
```

### 3.2.5 Composition

The *n-composition* or simply the *composition* of $n$ key-objects K1, K2, ..., K$n$ is a key-object formed as the set of key-objects K1, K2, ..., K$n$, where if some of key-objects K1, K2,..., K$n$, coincide, we rename them so that the resulting set is always composed of $n$ elements.

For example, the composition of atomic key-objects BRAND and MODEL is the set:

```
Comp(BRAND, MODEL) = {BRAND, MODEL}
```

The composition of three atomic key-objects BRAND, MODEL, and PRICE is the set:

```
Comp(BRAND, MODEL, PRICE) = {BRAND, MODEL, PRICE}
```

Because the result of the composition operation is a set, the composition is a commutative operation – the same operands taken in any order produce the same key-object. For example,

```
Comp(BRAND, MODEL, PRICE) = Comp(MODEL, BRAND, PRICE)
```

According to the definition of the composition operation, every non-atomic key-object is the composition of key-objects it contains as elements. For example, PRINT_RESOLUTION is a composition of RESOLUTION_H_DPI and RESOLUTION_V_DPI as follows:

```
PRINT_RESOLUTION = Comp(RESOLUTION_H_DPI, RESOLUTION_V_DPI)
```

Analogously, PRINTER_B is the composition of its elements as follows:

```
PRINTER_B = Comp(DUPLEX_MODE , MANUFACTURER , MODEL , PRICE ,
                 PRINT_RESOLUTION , PRINT_SPEED_B_PPM , PRINTING_METHOD)
```

The simplest case of composition is the *unary* composition, which involves a single operand and happens to have an interesting utility for multivalued key-object instances, as we shall see in the succeeding sections. For example,

```
Comp(BRAND) = {BRAND}
```

### 3.2.6 Composition Naming Convention

It may be useful to be able to "automatically" generate names for key-objects, produced as results of the composition operation. Therefore, we introduce the following naming convention.

Let N1, N2, …, N$n$ be a lexicographically ordered sequence of words, which are the names of key-objects K1, K2, …, K$n$, respectively. Then the word representing the name of the key-object produced as the composition of K1, K2, …, K$n$, is constructed from the names N1, N2, …, N$n$, and the alphabet symbols "ɾ", "ɹ", and "|" as follows:

$$[N1|N2|\dots|Nn]$$

For example, the composition of PRICE and BRAND, in any order, is named using the word:

```
[BRAND|PRICE]
```

Using this generated name, we can write,

```
[BRAND|PRICE] = {BRAND, PRICE}
```

And also,

```
[BRAND|PRICE] = {PRICE, BRAND}
```

As mentioned in the previous section, any nonatomic key-object is the composition of its elements. Therefore, the names of nonatomic key-objects from the catalog can be viewed as shorthand notations for the names generated using the composition naming convention. For example, PRINT_RESOLUTION can be viewed as shorthand for the following generated name:

```
[RESOLUTION_H_DPI|RESOLUTION_V_DPI]
```

Analogously, the name of PRINTER_B key-object is equivalent to the following generated name:

```
[DUPLEX_MODE|MANUFACTURER|MODEL|PRICE|
        |PRINT_RESOLUTION|PRINT_SPEED_B_PPM|PRINTING_METHOD]
```

Replacing the name of PRINT_RESOLUTION with its generated equivalent, we get another generated name for PRINTER_B key-object, as follows:

```
[DUPLEX_MODE|MANUFACTURER|MODEL|PRICE||PRINT_SPEED_B_PPM
        |PRINTING_METHOD|[RESOLUTION_H_DPI|RESOLUTION_V_DPI]]
```

Note that the position of the name

```
[RESOLUTION_H_DPI|RESOLUTION_V_DPI]
```

is different from the position of the name PRINT_RESOLUTION within the former generated name of PRINTER_B due to the lexicographic ordering requirement of the composition naming convention.

The last example is the composition naming for nonatomic key-object,

```
{BRAND}
```

produced as the unary composition of atomic key-object BRAND, as follows:

```
[BRAND]
```

*Note*: For the composition naming convention to work, the alphabet symbols " ⌈ ", " ⌉ ", and " | " must not be used in the names of the base key-objects.

## 3.3 CATALOGS ARE KEY-OBJECTS

Catalogs as sets of key-objects may themselves be considered key-objects. The hierarchy can go up to super-catalogs – that is catalogs of catalogs, which again are key-objects, and so forth. Though structurally equivalent, catalogs and key-objects may be treated differently in applications. For example, in KeySQL, key-objects are immutable, but catalogs are mutable – they can be changed by adding or removing key-objects.

## 3.4 INSTANCES AS HEREDITARILY-FINITE SETS

The instances of all key-objects are *pairs*, that is, sets consisting of two elements. One element of the pair is always a word representing the key-object name followed by the colon symbol ":", and another element is either a word or a set representing the key-object *value*. The values of atomic key-objects are words, and the values of nonatomic key-objects are sets.

For example, the following pair represents an instance of atomic key-object DUPLEX_MODE of the Mary's printer specification.

```
{DUPLEX_MODE:,0}
```

The sets representing values of nonatomic key-objects are structured like the respective key-objects, where each comprised key-object is replaced by a pair consisting of the key-object name and value. For example, the following pair is an instance of nonatomic key-object PRINT_RESOLUTION from our catalog.

```
{PRINT_RESOLUTION:, { {RESOLUTION_H_DPI:,600},
                      {RESOLUTION_V_DPI:,600} }
}
```

The following is a pair representing an instance of PRINTER_B key-object:

```
{PRINTER_B:,{ {DUPLEX_MODE:,0},
              {MANUFACTURER:,NULL},
              {MODEL:,A1},
              {PRICE:,99.99},
              {PRINT_RESOLUTION:,
                { {RESOLUTION_H_DPI:,600},
                  {RESOLUTION_V_DPI:,600} } },
              {PRINT_SPEED_B_PPM:,14},
              {PRINTING_METHOD:,LASER} }
}
```

*Note*: We only consider key-object names that do not contain the colon symbol ":", which is used to distinguish between the names and the values.

### 3.4.1 Multivalued Instances

Key-objects as sets cannot contain the same key-object at the same level more than once. And for the same reason, a key-object instance cannot contain the same instance of a key-object at the same level more than once. However, we did not address the question if a key-object instance may contain more than one instance of a key-object at the same level, if the instances have different values.

In fact they may, and we call such instances *multivalued*. For example, consider key-object SEASONS that consists of the set containing an atomic key-object SEASON as follows:

```
SEASONS = {{SEASON}}
```

Now, consider the following multivalued instance of key-object SEASONS:

```
{SEASONS:, { {SEASON:, WINTER},
             {SEASON:, SUMMER} }
}
```

In the next example, key-object NAMES includes two sets consisting of atomic key-objects: FIRSTNAME and LASTNAME, respectively, as follows:

```
NAMES = {{FIRSTNAME}, {LASTNAME}}
```

Then, the following example of a multivalued instance can represent the case when a person is known under more than one name.

```
{NAMES:, { {FIRSTNAME:, JAMES},
           {LASTNAME:, DOE},
           {LASTNAME:, MORIARTY} }
}
```

Suppose now that key-object NAMES is defined as consisting of a two-element set of the same atomic key-objects as above, as follows:

```
NAMES = { {FIRSTNAME, LASTNAME} }
```

Then, its multivalued instances can preserve information about the combinations of first and last names used by a person, as follows:

```
{NAMES:, { { {FIRSTNAME:, JAMES}, {LASTNAME:, DOE} },
          { {FIRSTNAME:, JAMES}, {LASTNAME:, MORIARTY} } }
}
```

### 3.4.2 Multiassumption

As we have seen in Section 3.4.1, multivalued instances can be useful for modeling practical use cases. However, when creating catalogs we may not know in advance what key-objects may have multivalued instances. And to create additional key-objects for the same entity in order to cover the single and the multiple value cases, like SEASON and SEASONS, can be cumbersome anyway.

Therefore, let us assume that for any key-object K of a catalog, there is always the key-object #K in the same catalog which is formed as the unary composition of K, that is, #K = {K}. For example, for key-object SEASON there is also key-object #SEASON as follows:

```
#SEASON = Comp(SEASON) = {SEASON}
```

This *multiassumption* immediately leads to infinite catalogs because for any original key-object K, we will have not only #K, but also ##K, ###K, etc. However, this does not seem to be a problem because hopefully the multi-multivalued instances are not needed very often, let alone the multi-multi-multivalued ones, etc.; and therefore, there is only the potential infinity of catalogs because we can add the hash tagged key-objects only when needed.

Consider the following examples of multivalued instances of key-objects produced by the multiassumption instead of using specially created key-objects SEASONS and NAMES.

```
{#SEASON:, { {SEASON:, WINTER},
             {SEASON:, SUMMER} }
}
```

```
{#NAME:, { { {FIRSTNAME:, JAMES}, {LASTNAME:, DOE} },
           { {FIRSTNAME:, JAMES}, {LASTNAME:, MORIARTY} } }
}
```

Multiassumption will be used in the definition of projection operation for key-object instances.

*Note*: Multiassumption excludes the hash sign "#" as the first symbol in the names of the original base key-objects of a catalog.

### 3.4.3 Flat Representation

A key-object is said to be *flat* if it consists only of atomic key-objects as elements. For example, key-object PRINT_RESOLUTION below is a flat key-object.

```
PRINT_RESOLUTION = {RESOLUTION_H_DPI, RESOLUTION_V_DPI}
```

An instance of this key-object has more levels of set nesting than the key-object itself, for example,

```
{PRINT_RESOLUTION:, { {RESOLUTION_H_DPI:,600},
                      {RESOLUTION_V_DPI:,600} }
}
```

However, we can spare some set nesting by representing the same instance in a different way, as follows:

```
{ {PRINT_RESOLUTION.RESOLUTION_H_DPI:,600},
  {PRINT_RESOLUTION.RESOLUTION_V_DPI:,600} }
```

This representation of a key-object instance is called *flat representation* and is defined as the set of instances of all atomic key-objects, which are *hosted* (contained at any level) by the original key-object. We use the qualified names to denote respective atomic key-objects. In this example, we only need one level of qualification, but generally more levels may be needed because a key-object may host an atomic key-object on more than one level.

We say that a key-object instance *allows flat representation* if and only if the instance can be reconstructed, given its flat representation and the key-object.

Not only the instances of flat key-objects allow flat representations. For example, consider the flat representation of our PRINTER_B instance as follows:

```
{ {PRINTER_B.DUPLEX_MODE:,0},
  {PRINTER_B.MANUFACTURER:,NULL},
  {PRINTER_B.MODEL:,A1},
  {PRINTER_B.PRICE:,99.99},
  {PRINTER_B.RESOLUTION_H_DPI:,600},
  {PRINTER_B.RESOLUTION_V_DPI:,600},
  {PRINTER_B.PRINT_SPEED_B_PPM:,14},
  {PRINTER_B.PRINTING_METHOD:,LASER}
}
```

In fact, any *single-valued* instance of any key-object allows flat representation. An instance is single-valued if it comprises no multivalued instances. Given a key-object and a flat representation of its single-valued instance, the original instance of the key-object can always be reconstructed.

In general case, the multivalued instances do not allow flat representations.

Consider the following multivalued instance of key-object `A={#B}`, where `B={X,Y}`.

```
{ A:,{{B:,{{X:,X1},{Y:,Y1}}},
      {B:,{{X:,X1},{Y:,Y2}}},
      {B:,{{X:,X2},{Y:,Y2}}}
    }
}
```

Its flat representation, by definition, should be formed as the set of the following elements:

```
{A.B.X:,X1},
{A.B.Y:,Y1},
{A.B.X:,X1},
{A.B.Y:,Y2},
{A.B.X:,X2},
{A.B.Y:,Y2}
```

Since the third element duplicates the first one, and the sixth element duplicates the fourth, we eliminate them and get,

```
{ {A.B.X:,X1},
  {A.B.Y:,Y1},
  {A.B.Y:,Y2},
  {A.B.X:,X2}
}
```

The original instance of key-object `A` cannot be uniquely identified by this flat representation because the following instance of the same key-object,

```
{ A:,{{B:,{{X:,X1},{Y:,Y1}}},
      {B:,{{X:,X2},{Y:,Y1}}},
      {B:,{{X:,X2},{Y:,Y2}}}
}
```

has the same flat representation.

```
{ {A.B.X:,X1},
  {A.B.Y:,Y1},
  {A.B.X:,X2},
  {A.B.Y:,Y2}
}
```

However, the following multivalued instance of the same key-object allows flat representation.

```
{ A:,{{B:,{{X:,X1},{Y:,Y1}}},
      {B:,{{X:,X1},{Y:,Y2}}}
     }
}
```

Its flat representation is constructed from the following elements:

```
{A.B.X:,X1},
{A.B.Y:,Y1},
{A.B.X:,X1},
{A.B.Y:,Y2}
```

Though the third element duplicates the first one and will be eliminated in the following flat representation, the original instance of the key-object A still can be reconstructed because there is only one choice for the second value of X of the original instance.

```
{ {A.B.X:,X1},
  {A.B.Y:,Y1},
  {A.B.Y:,Y2}
}
```

As an exercise, the reader can try to provide the exact characterization of the class of multivalued key-object instances allowing flat representations.

## 3.5 OPERATIONS ON KEY-OBJECT INSTANCES

Operations on key-object instances are only meaningful when they produce valid key-object instances. Particularly, traditional set operations of union, intersection, and difference when applied to key-object instances as sets do not generally produce valid key-object instances.

In this section, we consider composition and projection operations and restriction function on key-object instances.

### 3.5.1 Composition

Let S1, S2, ..., S$n$ be instances of key-objects K1, K2, ..., K$n$, respectively. Then the *composition* of the instances S1, S2, ..., S$n$ is the instance of the composition of K1, K2, ..., K$n$, where the instance of K1 is equal to S1, the instance of K2 is equal to S2, and so forth.

In the next example, we use the key-object composition naming convention.

Consider the following instance S1 of key-object PRICE.

```
{PRICE: ,99.99}
```

And, let the instance S2 of key-object MODEL be as follows:

```
{MODEL: ,A1}
```

Then, their composition,

```
Comp(S1,S2)
```

is the following instance of key-object [MODEL|PRICE].

```
{ [MODEL|PRICE]:, { {MODEL:,A1},{PRICE:,99.99} }
```

### 3.5.2 Projection

Let a key-object, A host only one occurrence of a key-object X. If there is only one X-instance in the A-instance or all X-instances within the A-instance have the same value, the *projection* of the A-instance on the key-object X is equal to the X-instance. If there are at least two different X-instances in the A-instance, the projection of A-instance on the key-object X is a multivalued instance of #X containing each of the X-instances. This definition is easily extended to the case of multiple occurrences of the key-object X in the key-object A because we can always qualify the occurrences to avoid ambiguity. To complete the definition, we postulate that if the key-object A does not host the key-object X, then result of the projection of any instance of A on X is the empty instance.

For example, the projection of our instance of PRINTER_B on key-object PRINT_RESOLUTION is equal to the instance of PRINT_RESOLUTION as shown next.

```
{PRINT_RESOLUTION:,{ {RESOLUTION_H_DPI:,600},
                     {RESOLUTION_V_DPI:,600} } }
```

When an instance is multivalued, its projection can also be multivalued. For example, the projection of our NAMES instance,

```
{NAMES:, { { {FIRSTNAME:, JAMES}, {LASTNAME:, DOE} },
          { {FIRSTNAME:, JAMES}, {LASTNAME:, MORIARTY} } }
}
```

on key-object LASTNAME is a multivalued instance of #LASTNAME as shown.

```
{#LASTNAME:, { {LASTNAME:, DOE},
              {LASTNAME:, MORIARTY} }
}
```

However, the projection of the NAMES instance on key-object FIRST-NAME is a single-valued instance shown next because the two instances of FIRSTNAME in the NAMES instance have the same value.

```
{FIRSTNAME:, JAMES}
```

Let us now extend the definition of projection operation to cover projections of key-object instances on multiple key-objects.

Let a key-object, A host key-objects X1, X2, ..., X$n$. Then the *projection* of an A-instance on the set of key-objects {X1, X2, ..., X$n$} is the instance of the composition of projections of the A-instance on each of the key-objects X1, X2, ..., X$n$. If the key-object A does not host all of the key-objects X1, X2, ..., X$n$, then the projection of any instance of A on the set {X1, X2, ..., X$n$} is the empty instance.

For example, consider, the projection of our instance of PRINTER_B key-object on the set of key-objects {MODEL, PRICE, PRINT_SPEED_B_PPM}, as follows:

```
{ [MODEL|PRICE|PRINT_SPEED_B_PPM]:,{ {MODEL:,A1},
                                     {PRICE:,99.99},
                                     {PRINT_SPEED_B_PPM:,14} }
}
```

Consider now the projection of our NAMES instance on the set of key-objects consisting of FIRSTNAME and LASTNAME. According to the definition, the projection is equal to the composition of projections of the instance on each of these key-objects. Therefore, the projection in question is as follows:

```
{ [FIRSTNAME|LASTNAME]:,{ {FIRSTNAME:, JAMES},
                          {#LASTNAME:, { {LASTNAME:, DOE},
                                         {LASTNAME:, MORIARTY} } } }
}
```

### 3.5.3 Restriction

Instance restriction is a predicate function that returns either *true* or *false* depending on the evaluation of a predicate on a key-object instance.

Let P be a predicate defined on the sets of instances of atomic key-objects from catalog C, and let K be a key-object from C. Let {A1, A2, ..., An} be the set of all atomic key-objects hosted by K, and let S be an instance of K. Then if the instance S is single-valued, the restriction R(S,P) of the instance S by the predicate P returns true when the predicate P is true on the set:

$$\{\{A1:, V1\}, \{A2:, V2\}, ..., \{An:, Vn\}\}$$

where V1, V2, ..., Vn are the values of the atomic key-objects A1, A2, ..., An, respectively, in the instance S. If the instance S is multivalued, the predicate is tested on all sets:

$$\{\{A1:, X1\}, \{A2:, X2\}, ..., \{An:, Xn\}\}$$

formed by combinations of values of X1, X2, ..., Xn of A1, A2, ..., An, respectively, in the instance S, where the first element of a combination is drawn from the values of A1, the second element is drawn from the values of A2, and so on. The restriction R(S,P) returns true when the predicate P is true on a set formed by at least one combination of values of A1, A2, ..., An in the instance S.

## 3.6 DATA STORES

Set-theoretic operations on key-object instances do not generally produce key-object instances. However, sets of instances are closed with respect to all set operations. In other words, the set-theoretic union, intersection, and difference of any two sets of key-object instances produce a set of key-object instances.

This observation may look trivial until we relate to the relational model where set operations on tables as sets of rows are only defined for relations having equal number of attributes of compatible types.

In this section we introduce a concept of *data stores* defined as the finite sets of instances of key-objects from the same catalog. A data store is then said to be *based* on this catalog.

Since all set-theoretic operations (and all other operations we consider) on the stores are total – that is, defined for any operands, any two data stores can be viewed as the parts of one and the same data store.

With respect to the relational model, data stores are analogs of tables and databases at the same time. Under this analogy, the same query could be addressed to all tables in all databases and the search result could be formed as the union of results returned from each table.

Some of the above only makes sense when the data stores are based on the same catalog, which guarantees the uniqueness of the key-object definitions, and this may seem to create a problem of maintaining a global catalog. However, it is not exactly the case because catalogs can be organized into super-catalogs, super-super catalogs, and so forth. Also, the synonymy relations allow for multiple key-objects with similar semantics to be mapped to each other under the query expansion. All of this can help dealing with the namespace upkeep.

### 3.6.1 Heterogeneous, Homogeneous, and Flat Stores

With respect to the structure of key-object instances contained in the data stores, the latter can be classified into various categories. Here, we distinguish *heterogeneous*, *homogeneous*, and *flat* data stores as follows:

- Heterogeneous data stores form the most general category within which a data store can contain instances of any key-objects at the same time.
- Homogeneous data stores are data stores that contain only instances of a single key-object.
- Finally, flat data stores are data stores that contain only instances of flat key-objects.

*Note*: Any heterogeneous data store can be viewed as the set-theoretic union of homogeneous stores. This observation will be used for the filtering operation on the stores.

### 3.6.2 Comparison with Relational Model

Table 3.1 relates the concepts of the key-object data model and the relational data model.

| Table 3.1  Key-Object Model Versus Relational Model | |
|---|---|
| **Key-Object Data Model** | **Relational Data Model** |
| Key-object | N/A |
| Flat key-object | Table schema |
| Key-object instance | N/A |
| Flat key-object instance | Table row |
| Heterogeneous data store | N/A |
| Homogeneous data store | N/A |
| Flat homogeneous data store | Table |
| Flat data store | Database |

## 3.7 OPERATIONS ON STORES

In Section 3.6, we stated that data stores, as sets of key-object instances, are closed with respect to traditional set operations of union, intersection, and difference. In this section, we formally introduce set-theoretic and special operations on data stores. The special operations are *filtering*, *projection*, *restriction*, *product*, and *join*, which, except for filtering, may be viewed as generalized analogs of the respective operations of relational algebra.

### 3.7.1 Union

The *union* of any two data stores A and B based on the same catalog is a data store formed as the set-theoretic union of the sets of key-object instances from A and B. That is, the union of A and B is the set consisting of all instances belonging to A or B or both. Note that the duplicate instances are eliminated.

### 3.7.2 Intersection

The *intersection* of any two data stores A and B based on the same catalog is a data store formed as the set-theoretic intersection of the sets of key-object instances from A and B. That is, the intersection of A and B is the set consisting of all instances belonging to both A and B. If A and B have no common key-object instances, the result of intersection is the empty store.

### 3.7.3 Difference

The *difference* of any two data stores A and B based on the same catalog is a data store formed as the set-theoretic difference of the sets of key-object instances from A and B. That is, the difference of A and B is the set consisting of all instances belonging to A and not to B.

### 3.7.4 Filtering

When discussing the classification of data stores we noted that any heterogeneous data store can be viewed as the set-theoretic union of homogeneous stores. The filtering operation allows to produce a substore of a given data store consisting exclusively of the instances of certain key-objects. These substores are called *store filters*. We use parenthesis notation to denote the store filters. For example, the following filter denotes a data store containing only the instances of key-objects `PRINTER_B` from data store `MyStore`.

```
MyStore(PRINTER_B)
```

The following filter example denotes a data store containing only the instances of key-objects `PRINTER_B` and `PRINTER_C` from data store `MyStore`.

```
MyStore(PRINTER_B, PRINTER_C)
```

The previous filter is the union of `MyStore(PRINTER_B)` and `MyStore(PRINTER_C)` as follows:

```
MyStore(PRINTER_B, PRINTER_C) = MyStore(PRINTER_B) + MyStore(PRINTER_C)
```

where the plus sign "+" denotes the union operation on stores.

### 3.7.5 Restriction

The restriction operation on stores is based on the restriction function for key-object instances. Namely, the *restriction* of a data store D by a predicate P is a store, which consists of all key-object instances S from D for which the instance restriction function R(S,P) returns true. For example, the Mary's printer query from Section 2.4.1 may represent a restriction of a store containing `PRINTER_B` key-object instances, where the predicate P is specified by the "where" clause of the query.

### 3.7.6 Projection

The projection operation for stores is based on the projection operation for key-object instances.

Namely, the *projection* of a data store A on a set of key-objects K is the set of projections of all key-object instances from A on the set K.

### 3.7.7 Product

The product operation for stores is based on the composition operation for key-object instances.

Namely, let D1, D2, ..., D$n$ be data stores based on the same catalog, then the *product* of the D1, D2, ..., D$n$ is a data store:

$$Prod(D1, D2, ..., Dn)$$

based on the same catalog and consisting of all compositions of instances,

$$Comp(S1, S2, ..., Sn),$$

where instance S1 belongs to D1, instance S2 belongs to D2, and so forth.

### 3.7.8 Join

Join is a useful operation of the relational data model. There are several types of join in the relational model, for example, inner joins and outer joins. The joins also differ in types of join condition, and the most common in this respect is equijoin, which is a join based on the equality predicate. All types of join have their natural analogs in the key-object data model.

A general definition of the join operation is as follows.

Let D1, D2, ..., D$n$ be data stores based on the same catalog, and let P be a predicate defined on the sets of instances of atomic key-objects from the same catalog. Then the *join* of data stores,

$$D1, D2, ..., Dn$$

by predicate P is the restriction of the product of the stores,

$$Prod(D1, D2, ..., Dn)$$

by predicate P.

# CHAPTER 4

# Structured Search Framework

*It is the framework which changes with each new technology and not just the picture within the frame.*

**Marshall McLuhan**

## 4.1 INTRODUCTION

This chapter introduces design principles, framework, and data architecture for structured search systems based on the key-object data model. These systems may vary widely depending on application areas, environments, data sources, and other factors. Not all design principles may be important or useful for all cases. However the presented general framework and data architecture aim to satisfy all listed principles, and designers of concrete systems can choose a mix of features they need to implement.

## 4.2 PRINCIPLES

The following principles of structured search systems are considered in this section:

1. Facts, not documents
2. Query independence
3. Search scalability
4. User control over search precision
5. User control over output order
6. Not only for humans
7. Security control
8. Real-time access

### 4.2.1 Facts, not Documents
Like in the database search paradigm, search results are structured and present factual data as opposed to documents or web pages, which essentially are texts in natural languages.

## 4.2.2  Query Independence

Structured queries are independent from data sources. To formulate a query, the query originators need not know from where the response may come, and even may be intentionally prohibited from knowing that, for example for security considerations. Nor do query originators need to know the number or the type of data sources that may participate or actually participate in answering the query.

## 4.2.3  Search Scalability

Heterogeneously structured data sources can be easily and routinely added to the system or dropped transparently for users.

## 4.2.4  Precision Control

The precision of structured search results depends exclusively on the query formulation as in the database query paradigm, and is not adversely affected by the number of data sources used by the system, as is the case with IR.

## 4.2.5  Output Order Control

The order of search results can be controlled by users via structured query interfaces as in the database query paradigm.

## 4.2.6  Not Only for Humans

The results of structured queries can be consumed by downstream systems or applications, and can also be originated programmatically by upstream systems or applications.

## 4.2.7  Real-Time Access

As in the database search paradigm, structured search can be performed in real time and the results can reflect the latest version of data available at the querying time.

## 4.2.8  Security Control

Neither search providers nor users necessarily have or need to have access to the complete version of data from which the search results are drawn.

## 4.3 GENERAL FRAMEWORK

### 4.3.1 Basic Functions

Basic functions of structured search systems can be generally described as follows:

1. Facilitate query origination by *users*
2. Deliver *queries* to *data providers*
3. Collect *responses* to the queries from the data providers
4. Deliver the responses to the query originators

### 4.3.2 Queries and Responses: Q-Format and R-Format

Queries are formulated in terms of key-objects using a structured query language *KeySQL* described in Chapter 5. Several query examples were in fact already presented in Chapter 2. The responses are sets of key-object instances that satisfy the queries.

Queries are delivered to data providers using a Q-format, and responses are received from data providers in an R-format. The Q-format is a machine-readable format designed for transporting KeySQL queries, and there can be various Q-formats. These can be based on XML or JSON making the Q-format both machine and human readable, and also compatible with a rich collection of already existing software. To minimize data traffic, binary file formats can also be used. Analogously, the R-format is designed to transport key-object instances.

### 4.3.3 Catalogs as Federating Namespaces

Structured search systems operate using common key-object namespaces provided by one or more catalogs. The namespaces are fully or partly shared with data providers, and different catalogs may be shared with different data providers. In general case, the systems expand the queries using catalog relations before sending them out to data providers. This means data providers can receive queries that do not require further expansion. Therefore, data providers generally need not be aware of the catalog relations or the original query formulations.

### 4.3.4 Data Providers

Data providers are service entities, which are supposed to receive queries in Q-format, process them, and return the responses in R-format. Data providers must be *registered* in order for the structured search system to interact with them.

### 4.3.5 Adding and Removing Data Providers

Generally, data providers can be added to the system or removed at any time; and the current set of data providers and their modes of operation are transparent for users.

### 4.3.6 Bus and Subscription Modes

There are two basic modes of operation for data providers: *bus* mode and *subscription* mode. In the bus mode, any query related to any key-object is sent to all registered data providers, and each provider can either answer the query or ignore it. In the subscription mode, data providers subscribe to support certain key-objects and only queries related to the supported key-objects are sent to the respective data providers. Generally, a mode of each data provider may be independent of the modes of other providers.

### 4.3.7 Query Processing by Data Providers

In order to support particular key-objects, data providers must have access to data sources reflecting the semantics of key-objects. This does not mean the data in the data sources are structured exactly as the key-objects. However, there must be certain correspondence between the source data semantics and the key-object semantics; otherwise, supporting a key-object by a data provider does not make much sense.

In other words, there must exist *mappings* between the source data and the supported key-objects. The mappings allow assembling key-object instances from the *native data* of the data sources and essentially function as the key-object views within the original data sources. However, implementing a mapping can generally be somewhat more complex than creating a view in a database. In the simplest case, the data may already exist in the form of instances of the supported key-objects.

Since KeySQL queries may not be directly interpreted by the data sources, the queries may need to be converted into scripts including one or more *native queries* supported by the data sources. This conversion can be automatic since the structural mappings are established.

After the native query scripts are executed, the resulting native data, if any, must be converted into the R-format of key-object instances, which are passed back to the system and eventually to the query originators.

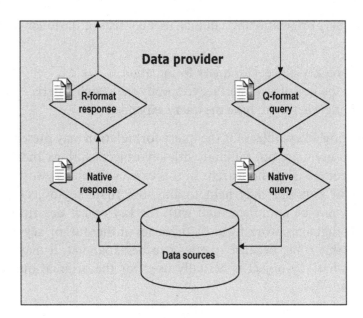

*Fig. 4.1. Query processing by data providers.*

The general scheme of query processing by data providers is shown in Figure 4.1.

Examples of data sources include SQL and NoSQL databases, XML document repositories, the sequence, record columnar, and other structured, semistructured, or unstructured file repositories residing at localized or distributed file systems, as long as the mapping into key-objects can be established and the Q-formatted KeySQL queries can be converted into the native queries.

Since the mappings may not be a one-to-one correspondence between the structures of key-objects and the native data of the particular data sources, some key-object instances received in response to the queries may contain incomplete information – some values may be NULL. At the same time, data sources may happen to contain data with a richer structure than the key-objects. This all is only natural when queries are independent from data sources.

### 4.3.8 Query Origination

Queries can be submitted to the system either via graphical user interfaces or via programmatic interfaces.

The query origination by a human user consists of the following principal steps:

1. Locating key-objects for query formulation
2. Using the key-object interface to specify the search criteria
3. Deciding whether to have the query expanded

Locating a key-object for the query formulation may present an issue when users are not familiar with key-object catalogs and/or with the subject areas of the search. In this case, a simple keyword search within the catalogs may help finding the right key-objects. Also, catalogs may be complemented with the key-object descriptions in natural languages, working as dictionaries or thesauri of key-objects. At the same time, because queries can be expanded, it may not be critical what key-object is actually used for the original query formulation.

### 4.3.9 Federative and Native Data Manipulation

In SQL terms, the only type of data manipulation provided by the framework is selection. Inserts, updates, or deletes make no sense in the general case. This mimics the functionality of IR where inserts, updates, or deletes cannot be performed via keyword interfaces.

Any additional processing of data returned in response to queries must be performed by the downstream applications outside the structured query protocol. Those applications may be included in services provided by the system. An example is "joining" the data returned in response to the queries by different data providers, or by one and the same data provider but from different data sources, or even from one and the same data source.

However in the case of native key-object data stores, all database functions make perfect sense. Particularly, KeySQL described in Chapter 5 has two semantics: *federative* and *native*. The native semantics allows for all traditional data manipulation statements, while the federative one includes only the selection.

Native data stores may complement federative search systems by providing storage mechanisms and enabling downstream processing of key-object instances returned by data providers.

### 4.3.10  Query Independence, Scalability, and Security

Structured queries in federative KeySQL do not contain "from" clause, as demonstrated by examples in Chapter 2 and also in Chapter 5. They only define the key-object structure of the response in "select" clause, along with the search criteria in "where" clause. The queries are not addressed to any particular logical or physical data source. This is the reflection of the query independence principle of the structured search.

The process of querying and receiving responses to the queries has no relation to the number of data providers or data sources that participate in answering the queries. New data sources or data providers can be added or removed at any time, or may just stop providing replies to all or some queries – all this is principally transparent for the users.

Users are isolated from data sources and cannot make any changes to the data. Only data providers have access to data sources and can decide what data may or may not be supplied for a given query or a given security context of a query. Neither users nor the federating system *per se* need to be aware of the structure or the content of the data sources, or to index the data sources in any way.

On the other hand, data providers generally may not know the identities of query originators but only may know security contexts of the queries. So, the framework is capable of enabling maximum security levels for both sides – the data providers and the users.

## 4.4  DATA STORE FUNCTIONALITY

Data stores have been formally introduced as sets of key-object instances. In this section, we consider their implementation as native key-object systems. Particularly, we review two groups of data store functions:

1. Catalog management
2. Store manipulation

Compared to the relational database systems, they play the role of data definition and data manipulation, respectively.

The catalog management functions are also necessary in the federative search framework and are supported by the federative KeySQL, as we shall see in Chapter 5.

## 4.4.1 Catalog Management

Catalog management functions include:

1. Creating and dropping catalogs
2. Creating and dropping key-objects
3. Creating and dropping synonymies (federative semantics)
4. Adding and removing objects to and from synonymies (federative semantics)

Let us note that synonymy relations can be defined as sets of key-objects – *synonyms* – and therefore the synonymies can be viewed as key-objects themselves, but more precisely, as catalogs. That is because the synonymies in KeySQL are mutable like the catalogs, while the proper key-objects are immutable. Synonymies can be modified by adding or removing synonyms, but the proper key-objects can only be created or dropped.

Besides the synonymies, other relations can be defined on key-objects, but we are not considering them here.

## 4.4.2 Store Manipulation

Store manipulation functions include:

1. Creating and dropping (data) stores
2. Inserting key-object instances into stores
3. Selecting key-object instances from stores
4. Updating key-object instances in stores
5. Deleting key-object instances from stores

Following the relational terminology, named data stores are called *base data stores* and the ones produced as results of operations on base stores are called *derived data stores*. For example, derived stores can be produced as results of selections from the base data stores.

Let us remind the reader that a data store can contain instances of multiple key-objects from a given catalog and any two data stores based on the same catalog can participate in any operation, like union, intersection, or difference, which produce a new data store. Data stores based on the same catalog are called *compatible*.

Any two compatible data stores can be viewed as parts of one and the same data store. This, in particular, enables flexible distributed architectures for high performance parallel processing of heterogeneously structured data.

# CHAPTER 5

# Introduction to KeySQL

*Language is only the instrument of science, and words are but the signs of ideas: I wish, however, that the instrument might be less apt to decay, and that signs might be permanent, like the things which they denote.*

**Samuel Johnson (A Dictionary of English Language – preface, 1755)**

## 5.1 OVERVIEW

KeySQL (*key-object structured query language*) provides SQL-like functionality for the key-object data model. The objective is to introduce the basic concepts of the KeySQL and to present the statements forming its skeleton, which can be further extended by analogs of many features of the standard SQL. Particularly, we don't address the data control functionality including user management with analogs of the GRANT or REVOKE statements. We also do not consider the transaction management. All that and many other features can be almost directly imported from the standard SQL and/or its proprietary flavors, as long as they are not materially specific for the data model itself. For the same reasons, we do not consider the concept of views. And finally, we leave out the issues of physical implementation that, though interesting in itself, would drive the presentation into somewhat different direction with respect to the objective of conceptual introduction. Some other limitations of the current presentation, as well as the possible extensions of the language are commented upon in the individual sections of this chapter.

### 5.1.1 CML and SML

We consider two basic parts of the language, as follows:

1. Catalog management language (CML)
2. Store manipulation language (SML)

Within the federative CML, we only consider the synonymy relations, though other relations can generally be considered as well.

There is also a set of SHOW statements as follows:

SHOW ATOMIC KEYOBJECT
SHOW NONATOMIC KEYOBJECT
SHOW CATALOG
SHOW SYNONYMY RELATION
SHOW KEYOBJECTS IN STORE

The SHOW statements provide the convenience of being able to re-view the definition or structural composition of the respective objects.

### 5.1.2 Federative and Native Sublanguages

KeySQL can be viewed as two sublanguages: *federative* and *native*. Both share a part of the CML, but the native CML does not include the concept of relations, and the native SELECT does not include the EXPAND functionality. The federative and native SML sublanguages have no shared statements, and the federative SML includes only the federative SELECT statement.

### 5.2 CATALOG MANAGEMENT LANGUAGE

CML includes the following statements:

CREATE CATALOG
DROP CATALOG
CREATE ATOMIC KEYOBJECT
DROP ATOMIC KEYOBJECT
CREATE NONATOMIC KEYOBJECT
DROP NONATOMIC KEYOBJECT
CREATE SYNONYMY RELATION
ADD TO SYNONYMY RELATION
REMOVE FROM SYNONYMY RELATION
DROP SYNONYMY RELATION

The following statements are only available in the federative KeySQL:

CREATE SYNONYMY RELATION
ADD TO SYNONYMY RELATION
REMOVE FROM SYNONYMY RELATION
DROP SYNONYMY RELATION
SHOW SYNONYMY RELATION

## 5.2.1 CREATE CATALOG

The statement has the following structure:

CREATE CATALOG <catalog name>;

### 5.2.1.1 Semantics

The statement creates a catalog with the specified name that can contain key-objects defined by the respective statements. A catalog is a set of key-objects that have been created in the catalog and have not been yet dropped from the catalog. In the federative KeySQL, the catalogs can contain synonymy relations, which also can be created in a catalog or dropped from it.

### 5.2.1.2 Example

```
CREATE CATALOG MyCatalog;
```

## 5.2.2 DROP CATALOG

The statement has the following structure:

DROP CATALOG <catalog name>;

### 5.2.2.1 Example

```
DROP CATALOG MyCatalog;
```

*Note*: Before a catalog is dropped, all data stores based on the catalog must be dropped.

## 5.2.3 CREATE ATOMIC KEYOBJECT

The statement has the following structure:

CREATE ATOMIC KEYOBJECT <atomic keyobject name> <type>

IN [CATALOG] <catalog name>;

In this introductory presentation, we consider only two types as follows:

NUMBER
CHAR

NUMBER means a fixed or floating-point number up to 38 decimal digits of precision.

CHAR means a character string of variable length up to 64 Kb. If the number of characters needs to be fixed, it is put in parenthesis after the CHAR specification. For example, CHAR(1) means a string of fixed length of one character, which is the minimal number allowed.

Only those two types are used in the examples. However, the set of types can be extended to cover the data types of the standard SQL or any of its proprietary flavors. For example, those can be Date, Time, Timestamp, BLOB, CLOB, etc.

### 5.2.3.1 Example

```
CREATE ATOMIC KEYOBJECT FirstName CHAR
IN CATALOG MyCatalog;
```

*Note on name uniqueness*: All names of atomic and nonatomic key-objects in a catalog must be unique.

### 5.2.4 DROP ATOMIC KEYOBJECT

The statement has the following structure:

DROP ATOMIC KEYOBJECT <atomic keyobject name>

FROM [CATALOG] <catalog name>;

*Note 1*: Before any key-object can be dropped, all key-objects having it in their definitions (CREATE NONATOMIC KEYOBJECT statements) must be dropped.

*Note 2*: When an atomic key-object is dropped, it is automatically removed from all synonymy relations it was added to.

*Note 3*: Before any key-object can be dropped, the substores defined by the key-object filter must be deleted from all data stores holding the instances of the key-object (using the DELETE statement).

### 5.2.4.1 Example

```
DROP ATOMIC KEYOBJECT FirstName
FROM CATALOG MyCatalog;
```

## 5.2.5  CREATE NONATOMIC KEYOBJECT

The statement has the following structure:

CREATE NONATOMIC KEYOBJECT <keyobject name> {<list of keyobject names>}

IN [CATALOG] <catalog name>;

Names in the list are the names of existing atomic or nonatomic key-objects separated by commas.

*Note on name uniqueness*: All names of atomic or nonatomic key-objects in a catalog must be unique.

*Note on order*: The order in the list is not significant and any two lists with the same set of key-object names are considered to be the same.

### 5.2.5.1 Example

```
CREATE NONATOMIC KEYOBJECT Name{FirstName,LastName}
IN CATALOG MyCatalog;
```

## 5.2.6  DROP NONATOMIC KEYOBJECT

The statement has the following structure:

DROP NONATOMIC KEYOBJECT <keyobject name>

FROM [CATALOG] <catalog name>;

*Note 1*: Before any key-object can be dropped, all key-objects having it in their definitions (CREATE NONATOMIC KEYOBJECT statements) must be dropped.

*Note 2*: Before any key-object can be dropped, the substores defined by the key-object filter must be deleted from all data stores holding the instances of the key-object (using the DELETE statement).

### 5.2.6.1 Example

```
DROP NONATOMIC KEYOBJECT Name
FROM CATALOG MyCatalog;
```

## 5.2.7 CREATE SYNONYMY

The statement has the following structure:

CREATE SYNONYMY [RELATION] <synonymy relation name>

IN [CATALOG] <catalog name>;

### 5.2.7.1 Example

```
CREATE SYNONYMY RELATION MySynonymy
IN CATALOG MyCatalog;
```

The CREATE SYNONYMY statement is only available in the federative semantics.

## 5.2.8 ADD TO SYNONYMY

The statement has the following structure:

ADD <list of atomic keyobject names>

TO SYNONYMY [RELATION] <synonymy relation name>

IN [CATALOG] <catalog name>;

The list includes one or more names of existing atomic key-objects separated by commas.

*Note*: Any atomic key-object can participate in only one synonymy at the same time.

### 5.2.8.1 Example

```
ADD Brand, Manufacturer
TO SYNONYMY RELATION MySynonymy
IN CATALOG MyCatalog;
```

The ADD TO SYNONYMY statement is only available in the federative semantics.

## 5.2.9 REMOVE FROM SYNONYMY

The statement has the following structure:

REMOVE <list of atomic keyobject names>

FROM SYNONYMY [RELATION] <synonymy relation name>

IN [CATALOG] <catalog name>;

The list includes one or more names of atomic key-objects separated by commas.

### 5.2.9.1  Example

```
REMOVE Brand
FROM SYNONYMY MySynonymy
IN CATALOG MyCatalog;
```

The REMOVE FROM SYNONYMY statement is only available in the federative semantics.

### 5.2.10  DROP SYNONYMY

The statement has the following structure:

DROP SYNONYMY [RELATION] <synonymy relation name>

FROM [CATALOG] <catalog name>;

### 5.2.10.1  Example

```
DROP SYNONYMY MySynonymy
FROM CATALOG MyCatalog;
```

The DROP SYNONYMY statement is only available in the federative semantics.

### 5.3  STORE MANIPULATION LANGUAGE

SML deals with stores, which are sets of key-object instances, and includes the following statements:

Federative SELECT
CREATE STORE
DROP STORE
Native SELECT
INSERT

UPDATE
DELETE
CREATE STORE AS SELECT
INSERT SELECT

The federative SML contains only one statement: Federative SELECT. All other statements from the above list belong to the native SML.

### 5.3.1 Syntax of Key-object Instances

The syntax of key-object instances is as follows:

<keyobject instance> ::= { <pair> }

<pair> ::= <keyobject name> : <value>

<value> ::= NULL | <char value> | <number value> |{<members>}

<members> ::= <keyobject instance> | <keyobject instance>, <members>

### 5.3.1.1 Examples

The following instance of atomic key-object DUPLEX_MODE,

```
{DUPLEX_MODE:,0}
```

has the syntactic representation:

```
{DUPLEX_MODE:0}
```

The following instance of the atomic key-object PRINT_RESOLUTION,

```
{PRINT_RESOLUTION:, { {RESOLUTION_H_DPI:,600},
                      {RESOLUTION_V_DPI:,600} }
}
```

has the syntactic representation:

```
{PRINT_RESOLUTION: { RESOLUTION_H_DPI: 600,
                     RESOLUTION_V_DPI: 600 } }
```

The following instance of nonatomic key-object PRINTER_B,

```
{PRINTER_B:,{  {DUPLEX_MODE:,0},
               {MANUFACTURER:,NULL},
               {MODEL:,A1},
               {PRICE:,99.99},
               {PRINT_RESOLUTION:,
                  {  {RESOLUTION_H_DPI:,600},
                     {RESOLUTION_V_DPI:,600} } },
               {PRINT_SPEED_B_PPM:,14},
               {PRINTING_METHOD:,LASER} }

}
```

has the syntactic representation:

```
{PRINTER_B:  {DUPLEX_MODE:0,
              MANUFACTURER:NULL,
              MODEL:'A1',
              PRICE:99.99,
              PRINT_RESOLUTION:
                 {RESOLUTION_H_DPI:600,
                  RESOLUTION_V_DPI:600},
              PRINT_SPEED_B_PPM:14,
              PRINTING_METHOD: 'LASER'}

}
```

## 5.3.2  JSON Representation of Instances

The KeySQL syntax of key-object instances introduced in Section 5.3.1 resembles the syntax of the java script object notation (JSON). For example, a JSON representation of our PRINTER_B instance may look as follows:

```
{"PRINTER_B":{"DUPLEX_MODE":0,
              "MANUFACTURER":"NULL",
              "MODEL": "A1",
              "PRICE":99.99,
              "PRINT_RESOLUTION":{"RESOLUTION_H_DPI":600,
                  "RESOLUTION_V_DPI":600},
              "PRINT_SPEED_B":14,
              "PRINTING_METHOD":"LASER"}

}
```

There are several major differences between the JSON syntax and the KeySQL syntax of the key-object instances. One of them is that the KeySQL syntax has only the "set" constructor represented by the curly braces, whereas JSON has also the array constructor. Another one is that a JSON object can be a set of pairs, whereas any KeySQL instance is always a pair. There are also other differences that we do not comment upon. However, the KeySQL instance syntax can be viewed as a subset of the JSON syntax if we abstract from some technicalities. This makes federation of heterogeneous data sources simpler because the translation from the KeySQL instance syntax into the JSON syntax and back can be pretty straightforward, and therefore JSON can serve as a natural data format for the transport of the key-object instances.

### 5.3.3 Federative SELECT

The statement has the following structure:

SELECT <list of keyobject names> |*

OF [CATALOG] <catalog name>

[WHERE <restriction predicate>]

[ORDER BY <list of atomic keyobject names, each followed by [ASC] or DESC >]

[EXPAND [<expansion algorithm reference>] ];

The comma-delimited list in the SELECT clause contains one or more names of key-objects defined in the catalog <catalog name>.

The asterisk "*" means "any key-object of the catalog."

The WHERE clause specifies a restriction predicate.

The list in the ORDER BY clause includes one or more names of atomic key-objects of the catalog <catalog name>, each followed by ASC or DESC and separated by commas. The ASC is the default option.

The EXPAND clause specifies an expansion algorithm, and when no expansion algorithm is specified the default one is used.

#### 5.3.3.1 Semantics

The statement returns an optionally ordered representation of an unnamed data store, which is formed as the set of instances of key-objects specified in the SELECT clause, for which the restriction function based on the predicate of the optional **WHERE** clause is *true*. The order of the output data store is specified by the optional **ORDER BY** clause.

If the **ORDER BY** clause is missing, the order of the output is generally implementation dependent. The **ORDER BY** clause has no effect if at least one key-object of the **ORDER BY** list is not contained by all key-objects, the instances of which form the resulting store. If the **ORDER BY** list references a multivalued key-object instance, the order is implementation dependent but can be specified using additional **ORDER BY** options, which are not considered here.

The **EXPAND** clause, if present, is processed during the query compilation and leads to possible generation of additional queries, which in turn have no **EXPAND** clause. The resulting data store is the union of all data stores produced by each of the generated queries and by the original query. The set of additionally generated queries depends on the expansion algorithm, the original query, and the catalog, including the relations. An expansion algorithm example is presented in Chapter 2, and is meant as the default one in the succeeding illustration.

### 5.3.3.2 Examples

```
SELECT printer_b
OF CATALOG MyCatalog
WHERE duplex_mode = 0
    AND resolution_h_dpi >= 600
    AND resolution_v_dpi >= 600
    AND print_speed_b_ppm >= 14
    AND printing_method = 'laser'
EXPAND;
```

```
SELECT *
OF MyCatalog
WHERE last_name = 'Moriarty';
```

```
SELECT printer_b
OF CATALOG MyCatalog
WHERE duplex_mode = 0
    AND resolution_h_dpi >= 600
    AND resolution_v_dpi >= 600
    AND print_speed_b_ppm >= 14
    AND printing_method = 'laser'
ORDER BY print_speed_b_ppm DESC, price_usd ASC;
```

## 5.3.4  CREATE STORE

The statement has the following structure:

CREATE STORE <store name>

FOR [CATALOG] <catalog name>;

### 5.3.4.1 Semantics

The statement creates a data store with the specified name that can hold instances of key-objects belonging to the specified catalog. A data store is a set of instances that have been inserted into the store. The data store is said to be *based* on the catalog <catalog name>. The catalog is said to be the *base* catalog of the data store.

### 5.3.4.2 Example

```
CREATE STORE MyStore
FOR CATALOG MyCatalog;
```

## 5.3.5  DROP STORE

The statement has the following structure:

DROP STORE <store name>;

### 5.3.5.1 Semantics

After the data store is dropped, it cannot be addressed by any statements of the SML. All key-object instances that were inserted into the data store are no longer accessible.

### 5.3.5.2 Example

```
DROP STORE MyStore;
```

## 5.3.6  Native SELECT

The statement has the following structure:

SELECT <list of keyobject names> |*

FROM <store name, filter, or store expression>

[WHERE <restriction predicate>]

[ORDER BY <list of atomic keyobject names, each followed by [ASC] or DESC >];

The comma-delimited list in the SELECT clause contains one or more names of key-objects of a catalog, which is the base catalog for all stores referenced in the FROM clause.

The names of key-objects can be qualified by the store names or aliases specified in the FROM clause, and can also be aliased. The optional AS reserved keyword is used to define the aliases.

The asterisk "*" means "no key-objects to project on."

The FROM clause contains an optionally aliased data store name, store filter, or store expression.

The filters are specified using the parenthesis notation defined in the Chapter 3.

The store expressions can be constructed from the store names and/ or filters using the following operators:

UNION
INTERSECT
MINUS
Product (represented as a comma-delimited list of store names, filters, or expressions).

The representation of the product as a comma-delimited list of operands follows the notation of the standard SQL.

The list in the ORDER BY clause includes one or more names of atomic key-objects of the base catalog, each followed by ASC or DESC and separated by commas. The ASC is the default option.

### 5.3.6.1 Semantics

The FROM clause specifies a data store and the optional WHERE clause specifies a predicate, by which the store is restricted according to the definition of the restriction operation on data stores. The optionally restricted data store is projected on the set of key-objects specified by the SELECT clause according to the definition of the projection operation on data stores. In the case of the asterisk in the SELECT clause, no projection is performed. The resulting set of key-object instances forms an unnamed data store. The statement returns an optionally ordered representation of this data store according to the order specified by the ORDER BY clause.

If the ORDER BY clause is missing, the order of the output is generally implementation dependent. The ORDER BY clause has no effect if at least one key-object of the ORDER BY list is not contained by all key-objects, the instances of which form the resulting store. If the ORDER BY list references a multivalued key-object instance, the order is implementation dependent but can be specified using additional ORDER BY options, which are not considered here.

### 5.3.6.2 Examples

Consider two data stores AmznStore and WlmrtStore. Then, the following SELECT statement creates an unnamed data store as the union of the filters of AmznStore and WlmrtStore on printer_c key-object and returns the projection of this data store on the set consisting of brand, model, and price key-objects. The result is presented in the ascending order of the values of price key-object instances.

```
SELECT printer_c.brand,
       printer_c.model,
       printer_c.price
FROM AmznStore(printer_c) UNION WlmrtStore(printer_c)
ORDER BY price ASC
```

Since the filter expression in the FROM clause specifies that only printer_c key-object instances will be projected, the qualified names for brand, model, and price key-objects can be replaced by the unqualified names with no ambiguity because each of these key-objects has only one occurrence in printer_c.

Therefore, the query can be rewritten as follows.

```
SELECT brand,
       model,
       price
FROM AmznStore(printer_c) UNION WlmrtStore(printer_c)
ORDER BY price ASC
```

The next two examples show the analogous queries where the IN-TERSECT and MINUS set operators are used instead of the UNION operator in the FROM clause.

```
SELECT brand,
       model,
       price
FROM AmznStore(printer_c) INTERSECT WlmrtStore(printer_c)
ORDER BY price ASC
```

```
SELECT brand,
       model,
       price
FROM AmznStore(printer_c) MINUS WlmrtStore(printer_c)
ORDER BY price ASC
```

The following query presents an example of equijoin allowing to compare printer_c prices from AmznStore and WlmrtStore. The FROM clause specifies the product of filters of the stores on printer_c key-object. The filters are aliased by the "a" and "w" names, respectively, with the optional AS keyword omitted. The restriction predicate of the WHERE clause specifies the join condition as the equality of the pairs of the brand and model key-object instances from AmznStore, and WlmrtStore, respectively. The SELECT clause specifies the projection on brand, model, and price key-object instances from the AmznStore and on the instance of price from WlmrtStore store. The latter two are aliased by the Amzn_price and Wlmrt_price names, respectively, using the AS keyword. The resulting unnamed data store will be presented in the ascending order of the respective prices.

```
SELECT a.brand,
       a.model,
       a.price AS Amzn_price,
       w.price AS Wlmrt_price
FROM AmznStore(printer_c) a,
     WlmrtStore(printer_c) w
WHERE a.brand = w.brand
  AND a.model = w.model
ORDER BY a.price ASC, w.price ASC
```

*Note on extensions*: The SELECT statement can be extended in several ways to make it more expressive. For example, the select clause could include not just the names of key-objects, but also the "value expressions" for the atomic key-objects that can be optionally aliased. For example,

```
(price + 0.1 * price) AS 'tax_price'
```

The analogs of the GROUP BY or HAVING clauses of the standard SQL can also be introduced. However, we are not considering these and many other possible extensions for the sake of simplicity and conforming to the general objective of conceptual introduction stated in the chapter overview.

### 5.3.7 INSERT

The statement has the following structure:

INSERT INTO <store name>

INSTANCES <list of key-object instances>;

The comma-delimited list of key-object instances contains one or more instances of the key-objects of a catalog, which is the base catalog for the store.

### 5.3.7.1 Example

```
INSERT INTO STORE PrinterStore INSTANCES
{PRINTER_B:  {DUPLEX_MODE:0,
             MANUFACTURER:NULL,
             MODEL:'A1',
             PRICE:99.99,
             PRINT_RESOLUTION:
                 {RESOLUTION_H_DPI:600,
                  RESOLUTION_V_DPI:600},
             PRINT_SPEED_B_PPM:14,
             PRINTING_METHOD: 'LASER'}
},
```

```
{PRINTER_B: {DUPLEX_MODE:1,
            MANUFACTURER:NULL,
            MODEL:'A2',
            PRICE:129.99,
            PRINT_RESOLUTION:
               {RESOLUTION_H_DPI:600,
                RESOLUTION_V_DPI:600},
            PRINT_SPEED_B_PPM:20,
            PRINTING_METHOD: 'LASER'}
},
{PRINTER_C: {DUPLEX_MODE:0,
            BRAND:NULL,
            MODEL:'C1',
            PRICE:139.99,
            PRINT_RESOLUTION:
               {RESOLUTION_H_DPI:600,
                RESOLUTION_V_DPI:600},
            PRINT_SPEED_B_PPM:16,
            PRINT_SPEED_C_PPM:10
            PRINTING_METHOD: 'INKJET'}
};
```

## 5.3.8  UPDATE

The statement has the following structure:

UPDATE <store name> |<store filter>

SET <set clause list>

[WHERE <restriction predicate>];

The <set clause list> is a comma-delimited list consisting of the following elements:

<atomic keyobject name>=<value expression> | NULL

### 5.3.8.1 Semantics

The UPDATE clause specifies a data store or a filter, and the optional WHERE clause specifies a predicate, by which the data store or the filter is restricted according to the definition of the restriction operation on data stores.

Each key-object instance of the restricted data store or the filter is updated by setting the values of instances of atomic key-objects from the SET clause list equal to the respective value expressions or to NULL.

If an atomic key-object name in the SET clause list is ambiguously qualified and/or its instances are multivalued, all the values of the atomic key-object are updated with the value of the respective value expression.

### 5.3.8.2 Examples

Consider PrinterStore data store containing key-object instances from the INSERT statement example. Then, the following UPDATE statement results in changing the monochrome printing speed information for the color printers satisfying the WHERE clause predicate.

```
UPDATE STORE PrinterStore
SET printer_c.print_speed_b_ppm = 25
WHERE printer_c.brand IS NULL
  AND printer_c.model = 'C1';
```

The same result can be produced by using a filter of PrinterStore on printer_c key-object. This allows avoiding all printer_c qualifications as follows:

```
UPDATE STORE PrinterStore(printer.c)
SET print_speed_b_ppm = 25
WHERE brand IS NULL
  AND model = 'C1';
```

The following UPDATE statement will result in increasing the price by 10% for all printer.b or printer.c instances in the PrinterStore.

```
UPDATE STORE PrinterStore
SET price = price + 0.1*price
```

### 5.3.9 DELETE

The statement has the following structure:

DELETE FROM <store name> |<store filter>

[WHERE <restriction predicate>];

#### 5.3.9.1 Semantics

The DELETE clause specifies a data store or a filter, and the optional WHERE clause specifies a predicate, by which the store or the filter is restricted according to the definition of the restriction operation on data stores.

Each key-object instance of the restricted store or the filter is deleted from the named data store.

If the WHERE clause is missing, all key-object instances are deleted from the data store or the filter.

#### 5.3.9.2 Examples

Consider the `PrinterStore` data store containing the key-object instances from the INSERT statement example. Then the following DELETE statement will result in deleting all instances of the color printers satisfying the WHERE clause predicate.

```
DELETE FROM STORE PrinterStore
WHERE PRINTER_C.PRINT_SPEED_B_PPM <= 16;
```

The following DELETE statement will result in deleting all instances of the monochrome printers from the `PrinterStore`.

```
DELETE FROM STORE PrinterStore(printer.b)
```

### 5.3.10 CREATE STORE AS SELECT

The statement has the following structure:

CREATE STORE <store name>

FOR [CATALOG] <catalog name>

AS <select statement>;

### 5.3.10.1 Semantics

Like the original CREATE STORE, the statement creates a data store with the specified name that can hold instances of key-objects belonging to the specified catalog. The data store is populated with key-object instances from the resulting data store of the SELECT statement presented after the AS keyword.

In particular, the statement allows for naming of the otherwise unnamed stores produced by SELECT statements.

*Note*: The FROM clause of the SELECT statement must reference only the data stores based on the same catalog as the one specified by the FOR CATALOG clause.

### 5.3.10.2 Example

```
CREATE STORE NamedStore
FOR CATALOG MyCatalog AS
SELECT *
FROM PrinterStore(printer.b) UNION MyStore(printer.c);
```

## 5.3.11 INSERT SELECT

The statement has the following structure:

INSERT INTO <store name>

<select statement>;

### 5.3.11.1 Semantics

The statement inserts all key-object instances from the resulting data store of the SELECT statement into the specified named data store.

*Note*: The FROM clause of the SELECT statement must reference only the data stores based on the same catalog as the one, on which the named data store is based.

### 5.3.11.2 Example

```
INSERT INTO NamedStore
SELECT *
FROM PrinterStore(printer.b) UNION MyStore(printer.c);
```

## 5.4 SHOW STATEMENTS

### 5.4.1 SHOW ATOMIC KEYOBJECT

The statement has the following structure:

SHOW ATOMIC KEYOBJECT <atomic keyobject name>

OF CATALOG <catalog name>;

It returns the definition of existing atomic key-object.

**5.4.1.1 Example**
The statement,

```
SHOW ATOMIC KEYOBJECT FirstName
OF CATALOG MyCatalog;
```

returns the following exemplary result:

```
CREATE ATOMIC KEYOBJECT FirstName CHAR
IN CATALOG MyCatalog;
```

### 5.4.2 SHOW NONATOMIC KEYOBJECT

The statement has the following structure:

SHOW NONATOMIC KEYOBJECT <nonatomic keyobject name>

OF CATALOG <catalog name>;

It returns the definition of existing nonatomic key-object.

**5.4.2.1 Example**
The statement,

```
SHOW NONATOMIC KEYOBJECT Name
OF CATALOG MyCatalog;
```

returns the following exemplary result:

```
CREATE NONATOMIC KEYOBJECT Name{FirstName,LastName}
IN CATALOG MyCatalog;
```

### 5.4.3 SHOW CATALOG

The statement has the following structure:

SHOW CATALOG <catalog name>;

It returns the current set of key-objects of the existing catalog in lexicographic order.

#### 5.4.3.1 Example

The statement,

```
SHOW CATALOG MyCatalog;
```

returns the following exemplary result:

```
CATALOG MyCatalog
{  FirstName,
   LastName,
   Name {FirstName,LastName}
};
```

### 5.4.4 SHOW SYNONYMY RELATION

The statement has the following structure:

SHOW SYNONYMY [RELATION]<synonymy relation name>

OF [CATALOG] <catalog name>;

It returns the current set of atomic key-objects of the existing synonymy relation in lexicographic order.

#### 5.4.4.1 Example

The statement,

```
SHOW SYNONYMY RELATION MySynonymy
OF CATALOG MyCatalog;
```

returns the following exemplary result:

```
SYNONYMY RELATION MySynonymy
OF CATALOG MyCatalog
{ Brand,
  Manufacturer
};
```

SHOW SYNONYMY RELATION statement is only available in the federative semantics.

## 5.4.5  SHOW KEYOBJECTS IN STORE

The statement has the following structure:

SHOW KEYOBJECTS IN STORE <store name>

FOR CATALOG <catalog name>;

It returns the lexicographically ordered set of key-objects, the instances of which are currently contained by the existing store.

### 5.4.5.1  Example

The statement,

```
SHOW KEYOBJECTS IN STORE PrinterStore
FOR CATALOG MyCatalog;
```

returns the following exemplary result:

```
KEYOBJECTS IN STORE PrinterStore
FOR CATALOG MyCatalog
{printer_b,
 printer_c
};
```

# CHAPTER 6

# Structured Search on Database Landscape

*Take in at once the landscape of the world,*
*At a small inlet, which a grain might close,*
*And half create the wondrous world they see.*

**Edward Young (Night Thoughts)**

## 6.1 QUESTIONS AND TOPICS

This chapter is motivated by questions and discussion topics from presentations of the structured search technology, key-object data model, and KeySQL. Its objective is to put the concepts introduced in the first five chapters into the perspective of the general database landscape formed after some 50 or so years of its development.

The points we address are as follows:

1. Key-objects and object-oriented programming paradigm
2. Key-object data model and object-oriented databases
3. KeySQL and NoSQL
4. Query independence and data independence
5. KeySQL and MPP architectures

## 6.2 KEY-OBJECTS AND OBJECT-ORIENTED PROGRAMMING PARADIGM

It is not unusual to receive the following question. Why introduce the concept of key-objects if there is already a well-known concept of object classes in the object-oriented programming?

The basic answer is that they are structurally not the same and carry different functional loads. The two major differences are as follows:

1. Each object class is principally independent of other object classes, except for the inheritance, which in this context is irrelevant. However, a nonatomic key-object can only be defined if all atomic

and nonatomic key-objects it consists of are already defined in the catalog. There is no catalog concept in the object-oriented programming. A catalog is a generalization of a database schema.

2. The second difference relates to manipulating objects in the object-oriented programming versus manipulating key-object instances. The former is carried out using methods, which are unary operations representing individual object behavior. The latter is carried out using operations on sets of key-object instances rather than the individual objects.

Besides avoiding obvious problems of using the same name for different concepts and some linguistic difficulties like speaking about "sets of classes", we of course, wanted to emphasize an important connotation between keywords and key-objects in the context of structured search. At the same time, we apologize to the object-oriented community for any inconveniences coming from our terminology while reading the book. For example, java developers may initially still think of classes and objects when dealing with key-objects and instances.

## 6.3 KEY-OBJECTS AND OBJECT-ORIENTED DATABASES

A typical question asked in this respect is as follows. It is well known that the object-oriented databases introduced in 1990s were unsuccessful; why another attempt?

The idea of object-oriented databases was brought into existence by the triumph of the object-oriented programming paradigm. The goal was to get rid of the "impedance mismatch" between the relational databases and the general-purpose programming languages by making the database data structures as rich as the data structures of the programming languages. Maybe this goal has been reached. The problem, as we see it, is that the baby has been thrown out with the bathwater. Let us explain.

A fundamental principle, which guided the progress in database systems and led to the relational databases, was "data independence." It basically means that logical and physical data structures are defined and exist outside application programs, which access the data stored and maintained in the databases.

In the case of relational model, due to its "Spartan simplicity", data independence brings the need of significant data transformations when moving data from the databases to the applications and back. These transformations are known to be detrimental for the overall system performance, and hence the impedance mismatch term.

However, for at least a couple of decades, the benefits of the relational model were seen as far outweighing the drawbacks, and this brought an overwhelming success to the relational databases. The main benefit is the high-level query languages, particularly SQL, which became the lingua franca for business analysts, and other business and program users.

Object-oriented databases aimed to get rid of the impedance mismatch, but also got rid of the high-level query languages, not offering anything in exchange and bringing some additional complexities of their own.

The key-object model is almost as capacious as the object-oriented one, so that the impedance mismatch can be avoided, but it provides the benefits of the high-level query languages with KeySQL being an example. Key-object data model does not have much in common with the concept of object-orientation, except for the shared word "object."

## 6.4 KeySQL AND NoSQL

It is not easy to speak about NoSQL because this term incorporates many different solutions. The typical meaning is that NoSQL movement defies the data independence principle just like the object-oriented databases did, and aims to provide an efficient and scalable application data store rather than a database in the traditional sense.

In the world of NoSQL, performance and reliability of the applications built on the commodity clusters is paramount, and there is no goal of supporting ad hoc querying or full-blown query languages. As long as the data objects, which may be pretty complex, can be reliably and quickly supplied to the application, the goal of the system is achieved. The data objects are typically retrieved via predefined access paths, for example using an object id, which could be multilevel. One example is retrieving a user account upon login.

If the relational databases were used to do the same, the time to join the normalized pieces of user data from different locations could be too long. Besides, the data must be replicated to multiple cluster nodes for scalability, reliability, and geographical affinity, especially in the systems that span the world. Doing the same using several pieces of data stored separately would be more complex and less reliable from the transactional viewpoint.

Like NoSQL, the structured search technology and KeySQL enable storing and retrieving complex data objects. However, KeySQL is a high-level query interface for manipulating sets of key-object instances rather than providing predefined access paths to individual objects for particular applications.

## 6.5 QUERY INDEPENDENCE AND DATA INDEPENDENCE

As mentioned earlier, the data independence principle guided the progress in database systems and led to the relational database technology. The key-object data model represents further evolution of the data independence principle relative to the relational model. It is achieved by using data objects of arbitrarily complex structure, which avoids the impedance mismatch, and by employing total operations on these objects.

The total operations in turn allow the applications to be less concerned with the distribution of data across the data stores because in the key-object data model, any number of data stores can be logically or physically combined into one data store or, vice versa, divided into multiple logical or physical data stores. So, the actual logical and/or physical composition of the data stores becomes more transparent for the applications that access them. The increased level of independence between data and applications also facilitates parallel and distributed data processing, which makes massively parallel processing (MPP) architectures an efficient natural choice for the implementation of native KeySQL databases.

In the federative setting, represented by the federative KeySQL, the data independence principle is replaced by the principle of query independence, which makes the logical and physical data structures of the data sources completely transparent for the human or programmatic query originators. Comparing the query independence of the structured search and the keyword search, let us note that structured search does not require any preindexing of the data sources in order for them to participate in the searches. It also enables the real-time data access because no preindexing is needed.

In the federative setting, there is no place for such traditional database functions as updates or deletes. This is a logical consequence of the query independence. On the other hand, foregoing the update and delete functionality in the federative setting provides the ultimate data security.

## 6.6 KeySQL AND MPP ARCHITECTURES

The response to the Big Data challenge is usually associated with MPP employing the shared-nothing architectures. This term typically relates to clusters of computers, each having its own memory and persistent data storage, whereas the computational power of the computers is combined for solving particular tasks. Common sense tells us that the way to deal with the exponential data growth is scaling out by using multiple "processors", each addressing its part of the stored data.

Of course, not all algorithms can be parallelized, but many can be to a certain extent. The goal is to employ data structures and algorithms that allow greater parallelization or, in other words, the greater share of the distributed data processing. The goal is typically considered to be achieved if an MPP system scales linearly for a given task, meaning the increase in the computer power brings the proportional reduction in the task processing time.

The "Spartan simplicity" of the relational model has its drawbacks with respect to the use of MPP architectures. One of them – the impedance mismatch – has been mentioned already. Another closely related one is the built-in need for the table joins, the operations that became widely known together with the relational databases. The joins generally do not scale linearly and because of that do not allow using the full power of MPP architectures. The less joins are needed for the query processing, the greater is the scalability. In the Big Data environment, the joins, along with the impedance mismatch, can pose serious performance challenges.

Whatever be the data model, the join operations reflecting the needs of combining information from different data sets may always be present in one or another form. But the use of joins can be minimized relative to the relational model if we avoid the necessity of some typical joins caused by the following intrinsic reasons.

1. Flat table structure and data normalization
2. Need for handling multiple values via joins

The first one was partially addressed in the context of impedance mismatch. Let us add that denormalization, which is often used for minimizing the number of joins, particularly in the online analytical processing (OLAP) systems, does not come free. It causes update anomalies and requires additional space when the same data is stored multiple times.

The second one is well known among developers who need to deal with modeling the business world realities that often produce multiple data values. Hence, the concepts of one-to-many and many-to-many relationships, and also the bridge, product, cross-reference, etc. tables, which are routinely joined because of the need of handling multiple values in SQL.

The key-object data model in the foundation of KeySQL makes it possible to avoid both types of joins induced by the relational model *per se* as stated earlier. It allows data objects of arbitrary complexity and also naturally incorporates multiple values of one or more key-objects within the hosting key-object instances. At the same time, KeySQL provides the analog of the relational join functionality in the key-object setting.

# CHAPTER 7

# Structured Search Solutions

*There is always an easy solution to every problem – neat, plausible, and wrong.*

H.L. Mencken

In this chapter, we consider structured search solutions, exemplary applications, and use cases.

## 7.1 E-COMMERCE APPLICATIONS

This section deals with applications and case studies of using the structured search technology in e-commerce.

### 7.1.1 Saving Millions of Hours to Shoppers

As mentioned in Chapter 1, the use of keyword search in e-commerce has several shortcomings. Particularly, it does not allow finding merchandise directly by specifications rather than by keywords like brand or model needed to retrieve product specifications. As a result, research of complex items may take hours and still does not guarantee the best deals. It would be vastly more efficient to search by multiple item characteristics at once instead of going back and forth through dozens or hundreds of descriptions in order to compare them by several parameters. There are billions of Internet users worldwide. How many hours do they collectively spend researching goods and services for a purchase? A conservative estimate would probably come to at least millions of hours a year.

The structured search technology allows to significantly reduce average time spent researching and comparing products online, especially for expensive items like computers, TVs, digital cameras, etc. The research can take minutes instead of hours. This means saving millions of hours wasted every year.

## 7.1.2 Optimizing and Energizing Marketplace

Another shortcoming of the keyword search is that the search output rankings are generally unrelated to the qualities of merchandise (i.e., specifications) or the deals offered. Since the search results tend to be voluminous, high search ranks are critical for merchants.

The keyword search puts buyers at a disadvantage because they are only able to look through the first few pages of an output, and whereas a better deal may be on the next page that they did not get to see.

When buyers can find the best deals faster and more reliably, the competition in the marketplace increases and the markets work more efficiently. Therefore, working to the buyer's advantage, the structured search technology enables better prices, better shopping experience, and a more efficient and energized marketplace at large.

## 7.1.3 Structured Search Advertising

Currently, search advertising is sold on the basis of auctioned keywords. For advertisers, keywords indicate consumer interests, and the intrinsic imprecision of keyword search means the intrinsic imprecision of advertising.

For example, let us recall Mary, who wants to buy a laser monochrome printer with certain specifications that cannot be efficiently expressed using keywords. In the keyword world, advertisers have little chance to reach Mary with ads pointing exactly to the class of printers she is looking for.

Within the structured search technology, the pinpoint accuracy of advertising can be easily achieved if and when desired. The intentions of consumers can be detected much more precisely because the structured search criterion is a much more accurate description of the buyers' intentions compared to just the "printer" keyword, for example. Therefore, the search advertising can be made much more cost-efficient for the advertisers.

At the same time, the structured search providers will have much more to sell. Instead of a single sale item like the "printer" keyword, they can sell numerous categories and types of printers defined as "spaces" of printer characteristics or parameters. Each time a structured query is submitted by a potential buyer, the search criterion can be analyzed in real time and compared to the spaces of printer parameters booked by the advertisers. If a match is determined, the ads of the respective advertisers will be shown.

### 7.1.4 Mobile E-Commerce

With its precision, the key-object search technology is especially well suited for the mobile e-commerce applications. This is not only because of smaller displays but also due to the on-the-go nature of the mobile users who generally may need faster access to information and have less time to sift through voluminous search outputs.

In particular, the technology enables e-merchants to store structured queries and execute them periodically for the interested buyers. The search results can be returned via email or text messaging. With the keyword search this does not seem practical because querying is not as precise and typically produces too big and noisy responses.

### 7.1.5 BayZon Marketplace

A giant Internet marketplace BayZon brings together buyers and sellers. There are three types of sellers: *Vendors*, *Small*, and *Tiny*. And the buyers are either *Active* or *Lazy*.

Due to stiff competition, the business slows down and BayZon aims to beat rivals by raising customer satisfaction. According to surveys, buyers spend a lot of time locating the right merchandise, especially for complex electronics like flat screen TVs, computers, digital cameras, and also many others.

There are two principle ways to locate an item at the BayZon website: either by classification or by keywords, neither allowing comparing multiple items. Besides, merchandise descriptions vary significantly in their structure and naming. The research of complex and expensive items may take hours and still does not guarantee the best deals. It is much more efficient to search by multiple characteristics of items simultaneously instead of going through dozens or hundreds of descriptions back and forth in order to compare them.

BayZon decides to use the structured search technology to get ahead of the competition. They start with picking several dozen most popular merchandise categories and creating a catalog of the respective key-objects.

The Vendors are skeptical. Their inventory databases are highly normalized and the item descriptions are scattered across the tables; also the data structures are different from the buyer-friendly BayZon catalog. However, IT finds a solution in a middleware that receives the BayZon queries in Q-format and translates them into the SQL queries to the databases. The responses are joined and returned to the BayZon systems using the R-format. The Vendors love to inject customized, precisely pointed ads into the search results, since the key-object queries accurately describe the buyers' needs.

The Small sellers do not have much of IT resources. Their inventories are relatively small and the data is kept in various ways including spreadsheets. They cannot provide online access to their systems or pay for the middleware. BayZon has a solution. The Small sellers supply the merchandise descriptions to BayZon using formatted files. BayZon creates simple software that converts the files into the R-format. The inventory readings and prices of the Small sellers are not real time; still their goods and ads fall into the same search results.

The Tiny sellers sell just a few things. BayZon asks them to load their data manually on the BayZon website like they did previously. The difference is that the item descriptions now match the catalog and the R-format. Thus, their goods and ads will also get into the same search results. The Tiny sellers are happy because now they need not invent how to best describe their merchandise for buyers to find it. They know their items and ads will be visible to the buyers on an equal footing with all other sellers.

The Active buyers search for the best deals because they like to do it or in order to buy cheap and resell. They research the market daily or even hourly. BayZon is ready to help and suggests storing their queries and running them periodically for the Active buyers. The search results are returned by email or text messages. Previously this was impossible because querying was not as precise as with the key-objects and produced too big and noisy responses.

The Lazy buyers do not buy every day and hate spending time researching stuff. Now they are happy because research takes just minutes.

They love BayZon and recommend it to all their Lazy friends, so the BayZon sales grow fast.

The experiment went well for BayZon, and even before the financial results were announced, their stock went up on the news about the new technology and a great new mobile e-commerce application they created. Now BayZon licenses their key-object catalogs and respective data formats to other companies and the whole marketplace becomes more and more organized and efficient for everyone.

### 7.1.6  BinYahGoo Search Portal

Following the success of the BayZon marketplace, the BinYahGoo search portal decides to revive their e-commerce search by exploiting the structured search technology. They go ahead and license the BayZon key-object catalog and add even more key-objects and relations.

For e-commerce BinYahGoo uses an in-memory database, which makes the structured search extremely fast. It also allows programmatic search interface that can be used by the partner sites directing traffic to BinYahGoo.

BinYahGoo offers their e-commerce search engine software for the local use by the retailers. In addition to the benefits of the excellent local search, the software also works as a web service providing a programmatic search interface to the retailers' websites. In particular, this allows BinYahGoo to use the interface for the real-time product search.

This real-time feature makes BinYahGoo e-commerce search engine even more popular with the users because it guarantees no stale information in the search results.

The reasonable investments paid off big. BinYahGoo became the leader in the e-commerce search. The traffic to the portal has increased significantly, and they easily made up for the year of commission free directing with the revenue growth from the search advertising.

Many more Internet retailers have signed up with BinYahGoo because they want their products and ads to appear in the best e-commerce search results in the industry.

A recognized leader in the e-commerce search, BinYahGoo provides excellent services and saves the customers millions of hours they used to spend on researching the merchandise and looking for the best deals.

## 7.2  SECURE FEDERATED SYSTEM

The government of the Great Country has many departments and agencies that maintain numerous databases containing valuable information. If the bits and pieces of information scattered across the databases were combined and made available for querying as a whole, the total value of data would be much higher, resulting in a significant advantage for the Great Country.

Unfortunately, this became even more evident due to a tragic event. Recently, the Great Country was attacked by terrorists and there were indications that the attack might have been prevented if information from several government databases could have been combined.

The government realizes the problem and looks for a solution. It decides to start by integrating a number of databases belonging to several agencies that were recently combined into the Super Agency. Besides the pure data integration problems, there are serious security issues to be addressed because of the sensitive nature of the data sources.

The Super Contractor hired by the Super Agency decides to use the structured search technology in order to build a scalable federated system allowing querying of heterogeneous data from multiple disparate sources in a secure manner. After consultations with the prospective users, an initial key-object catalog is created. It includes synonymy relations and also other relations specific to the nature of the system. The structured queries in Q-format can be originated using either a graphical user interface or a programmatic interface.

A brief description of the system is as follows. The key-object catalog is classified. Users log in under secure identities. Each secure identity belongs to one or more classes of security. Depending on the security class, users may see and use only certain subsets of the key-object catalog. Each query is assigned a security context that depends on the security class of the query originator and other factors.

The data provider entities operate in one of two modes: a gray box or a black box.

The gray boxes use the subscription mode. Their information profiles are the sets of key-objects they support, so that only queries relating to those key-objects will be routed to the gray boxes. The information profiles of the data providers are classified.

The black boxes use the bus mode: all queries come to the black boxes, which deal with them on their own. All other functions are the same for the gray and black boxes.

When a box receives a query, it checks out the security context. Depending on the security context and the relevance of the query, it may be ignored, or some response data may be obscured or not included in the response, or other actions may be taken.

The responses are built as follows: Q-format queries are converted into scripts comprising the native queries. The native queries are executed against the data sources. The native responses are assembled into R-format and returned to the query originators. The identities of the data providers and data sources in the response messages are obscured by the secure communication network.

The system has successfully passed all tests and was accepted. It is now being extended with new data providers and data sources. The key-object catalog is being enriched with new key-objects and relations. Soon, potentially all government data sources of the Great Country could be simultaneously and securely searched with a single query.

## 7.3  NATIVE KeySQL SYSTEMS

In this section, we consider some native KeySQL *applications*. The list is by no means comprehensive but is intended to illustrate the typical benefits that can be brought by the use of structured search technology in the form of native key-object data stores.

### 7.3.1  Healthcare Information Systems

We consider the healthcare applications not just because they are positioned to benefit from the use of the structured search technology and

KeySQL, but also as a representative of a class of such applications, which have common issues with respect to their relational database implementations.

As a background, let us mention that after more than 45 years from the beginning of the relational era, there are still prerelational medical systems in use. This illustrates not just the conservative nature of the healthcare subject area, but also the probable fact that the conversion of those systems to the relational platform did not look overwhelmingly advantageous.

For the sake of brevity, let us point to just two principal characteristics of the healthcare information systems as follows:

1. The healthcare data objects tend to be relatively complex and variable in their structure and contain multiple groups of multivalued attributes. For example, a patient can have multiple diagnoses, each of which can require multiple medications, etc.
2. There is an underlying design requirement of supporting the electronic exchange of the health records between the different systems.

Both support the idea that the key-object data model and KeySQL can be more appropriate than the relational model and SQL for use in the healthcare applications.

Particularly, the key-object model drastically reduces the number of related data records needed for representing a clinical case compared to the relational model. This simplifies and speeds up the ad hoc querying of the related data and combining it into the comprehensive information objects, particularly for the data exchange purposes. The reverse process of inserting the information from the incoming electronic exchange messages into the receiving systems also becomes more straightforward and quick.

The natural compatibility of the key-object instance syntax with the JSON based data transport formats can bring additional advantages.

Data warehousing of healthcare information and subsequent analytical processing and reporting can also benefit from the use of the key-object data model and KeySQL. The supporting arguments are in line with those presented in Section 7.3.2, dedicated to data warehousing.

### 7.3.2 Big Data Warehousing

Data warehousing is a field of database applications that received its recognition and wide acceptance some 20 years after the relational databases were invented. Since that time, the data warehouses became an important and valuable part of almost any IT organization.

Unlike the operational systems, which typically use a relatively small set of predefined data access paths, the data warehousing applications require the full-scale use of structured query languages, particularly SQL, which currently has little competition in this area.

The intrinsic part of the data warehousing technology are the processes collectively known as extract, transform, and load (ETL), which are used to extract data from the operational systems and load it into the data warehouses for subsequent analytical processing.

The ETL procedures typically involve moving around large amounts of data, and are performance-hungry. This is especially true when the Big Data must be analyzed as fast as possible in order to extract information critical for tactical and strategic business insights.

NoSQL systems are successfully competing with SQL databases for their use in operational systems. However, the data warehousing still remains mostly the SQL domain because the use of SQL and particularly the use of ad hoc queries, is so far basically irreplaceable for the business users.

That is why at least part of the data produced by the NoSQL systems is eventually loaded into the SQL data warehouses for analytical processing. At the same time, it is already clear that the performance of ETL procedures and SQL databases become more and more inadequate for digesting the Big Data.

The critical path of the Big Data warehousing is determined by the following main issues.

1. The data from the NoSQL operational systems need significant transformations in order to be loaded into multiple relational tables. This makes it difficult to fit the ETL processes into the batch windows, and leads to the principle inability of loading all data that may be potentially beneficial for gaining the business intelligence.

In reality, the percent of Big Data that can be timely and reliably loaded into the SQL data warehouses is diminishing with time as the Big Data grows along the dimensions of the three V's.

2. The performance of even pretty big and expensive SQL databases puts limits on the ability to process the ever-growing data volumes. The most problematic part of this processing is joining big tables. In Chapter 6, we have already mentioned that the joins are generally difficult to parallelize. But the relational technology heavily relies on the joins because of its inability to handle multiple data values and data normalization, which in turn is caused by the need to avoid the update anomalies and the excessive storage volumes.

The structured search technology based on the key-object data model and implemented in the native KeySQL data stores is on the one hand compatible with the rich data objects of the NoSQL operational systems, and on the other hand provides functional equivalent of the SQL querying capabilities. This makes it a better choice for the Big Data warehousing than the relational database technology.

The use of KeySQL stores would allow speeding up the ETL processes because the lossless data transformations from the NoSQL models into the key-object model are generally much more straightforward. At the same time, the ad hoc querying capabilities of the KeySQL are comparable with those of the SQL, as basically entire SQL functionality can have its analogs in the KeySQL. Performance-wise, KeySQL has an advantage of reducing the relative share of joins that hamper the overall performance of the SQL data warehousing solutions.

### 7.3.3 KeySQL on MapReduce Clusters

The key-object data model is more capacious and general than the relational one. And it is also more scalable. As mentioned in Chapter 6, though KeySQL supports the analogs of the relational join operations, it eliminates the intrinsic necessity of joins caused by the flat table structure and the need for handling multiple values via joins. As a result, the share of join operations in the KeySQL query processing is reduced relatively to the relational model. At the same time, the share of restriction operations is increased. This is because, unlike the relational model, complex data objects with multiple values are native to KeySQL, so the restriction predicates are evaluated directly on the base key-object instances instead of first collecting their parts from multiple tables via joins. Minimizing the share of joins and maximizing the share of restrictions allow KeySQL systems to take better advantage of the MPP shared-nothing architectures since the restrictions always scale linearly, while the joins generally do not.

Unlike the relational restriction, its key-object analog is a total operation. Its definition allows any key-object instance based on a given catalog as the argument, while the relational restriction is bound by the table schema. This facilitates associative access to key-object data and promotes scalability.

A general property of the key-object data model that makes it inherently more scalable than the relational one is called "additivity" and relates to the function of data accumulation. Suppose something is called "data." Then, there must be an operation of adding or combining the data. The question is what is the result of adding data to data. The intuition says that the result must be data as well. In other words, if A is data, and B is data, then A + B (and B + A) must be data, where the plus sign "+" denotes the operation of data accumulation. Let us call the data model additive if the "+" operation has the following properties:

1. Idempotence: A + A = A
2. Associativity: A + (B + C) = (A + B) + C
3. Commutativity: A + B = B + A

Note that the mentioned properties should be valid for any "data." So, the "+" operation is total with respect to whatever we call data.

The data accumulation operation of the key-object model is the union operation on the data stores. Namely, the union of any two data stores (based on the same catalog) is a data store. Of course all other set operations on the data stores are total as well, and generally all operations on the data stores we have considered are total.

This is not the case for the relational model, where the union of two relations, as well as all set operations on the relations, is partial. They are only defined for the union-compatible relations, which are the relations having equal number of attributes of compatible types. So, the relational model is only partially additive.

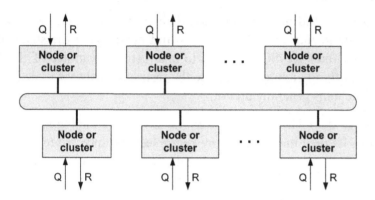

*Fig. 7.1. Structured search cluster.*

The properties of the key-object data model enable highly scalable implementations of the native KeySQL databases using predominantly or exclusively associative access to data. Those implementations can use computer clusters having, by orders of magnitude, more nodes than any contemporary SQL MPP systems.

Particularly, the MapReduce framework over the distributed file systems provides a natural foundation for the cluster KeySQL implementations. Figure 7.1 illustrates the architecture of such "stackable" structured search clusters integrated by the common namespaces of key-object catalogs, where each node can be a cluster of its own, receiving the queries and returning the responses.

## 7.4 STRUCTURED SEARCH IN INTERNET EVOLUTION

Though modern life is unimaginable without it, the Internet came into being only a couple of decades ago. And even though the technology evolves with ever-increasing acceleration, we are just in the very beginning of the Internet development spiral. This observation is fully applicable to all contemporary Internet applications including search, which is synonymous with keyword search at the time of writing. Here, we present some ideas on how today's keyword search can be complemented with the structured search as the Internet matures.

### 7.4.1 Internet as Data Store

To start with, let us imagine that in some not so distant future, the meaning of documents or web pages could be programmatically extracted from their texts in natural languages and presented in the form of structured data that can be consumed by computers. Then, these structured data objects can be routinely produced by search engines using some "semantic" indexing algorithms, much like they currently produce the keyword presentations of web pages using full-text indexing. The structured data objects representing the sense of the web pages can then be stored in databases, which would enable searching by meaning rather than by keywords. The result of such semantic search would be factual information rather than mere links to web pages, which may or may not contain the information.

Following this scenario, it is plausible that initially semantic indexing algorithms would not be fast enough to index the web in reasonable time. Then, the website originators can prepare structured data objects describing the sense of their web pages and link or embed them into the respective web pages. So, search engines would just collect the structured data objects along with the web pages instead of generating them on their own.

In fact, similar processes used to take place with keywords before the age of the full-text automatic indexing. Early IR systems did not have enough intelligence, power, or storage for the full-text automatic document indexing routinely performed by the contemporary search engines. Instead, manual indexing procedures were used to assign the keywords or descriptors to documents. For example, the keywords would be provided by authors of books or scientific articles. Alternatively, designated specialists would perform indexing and create document representations enabling keyword search.

The structured data objects in question could possibly be called something like "semantic key-objects" as they would function analogously to keywords but enable finding facts rather than documents. Key-objects, which are the subject of this book, perform the same function. The only thing missing with respect to the bright future of the search engine technology we have painted is robust algorithms of extracting meaning from texts in natural languages. Scientists are still working to deliver them.

However, there is no need to wait for this missing piece to start enjoying the fruits of the technology right now instead of putting it on hold till the good future times. Same as the keywords in the IR systems, we

| Monochrome Printer |  |
| --- | --- |
| **BEST VALUE!** |  |

| Price USD | 99.99 |
| --- | --- |
| Manufacturer | Unknown |
| Model | A1 |
| Printing Method | Laser |
| Duplex Printing | No |
| Max Print Speed Black, ppm | 14 |
| Max Print Resolution, dpi HxV | 600x600 |

*Fig. 7.2. Web page describing a monochrome printer.*

can supply key-objects to search engines by linking or embedding them into web pages.

For example, we can attach instances of our favorite PRINTER_B key-object to e-commerce web pages describing monochrome printers, so that Mary and others could easily and quickly find them using search engines with structured user interfaces.

Consider the following exemplary web page describing a mono-chrome printer at some e-commerce site as shown in Figure 7.2. Now, consider the abbreviated HTML source of the same web page shown in Figure 7.3. The HTML source contains an exemplary meta-tag "keyob-jects" with a link to an exemplary JSON file "filename.json" containing the instance of the key-object PRINTER_B shown at the Figure 7.4.

Generally, multiple meta-tags "keyobjects" may be included in the web page, each pointing to a file containing single or multiple instances of one or more key-objects. Alternatively, the meta-tag can point to a linked file containing multiple instances of multiple key-objects.

The previous example relates to the case when a representation of a key-object instance is linked to a web page. Alternatively, a representation

```
<!DOCTYPE html>
<html>
<head>
<meta http-equiv=Content-Type content="text/html; charset=UTF-8" />
<meta name="keyobjects" content="filename.json"/>
</head>
<body lang=EN-US>
<div class=WordSection1>
    <p><b><span style="font-family: Courier">Monochrome Printer</span></b></p>
    <p><span style="font-size: 16.0pt">BEST VALUE!</span></p>
    <table width="720" border="1" cellpadding="2" cellspacing="0">
        <tr>
            <th scope="row"><b><u><span style="font-family: &quot;Arial&quot;, &quot;sans-serif&quot;">Price
USD</span></u></b></th>
            <td><b><span style="font-family: Courier">99.99</span></b></td>
        </tr>
...
```

*Fig. 7.3.  Abbreviated HTML of the web page.*

of the same instance can be embedded directly into the web page. However, the linking technique seems to be more flexible and does not increase the size of the web page sources.

We can do the same with all other goods and services presented at e-commerce websites. Search engines could collect key-object instances along with their respective web pages, store, and use them to provide the structured search capabilities. They can also in real time analyze Key-SQL queries produced by the structured end-user query interfaces in order to inject precisely targeted advertisements into the search results.

Of course, e-commerce is just an example of one area where structured data objects in the form of key-object instances can be used to enable the structured search. There is virtually no limit to applications that can benefit from this technology. We believe that transformation into a global data store is a logical step in the Internet evolution.

```
{"PRINTER_B":{"DUPLEX_MODE":0,
              "MANUFACTURER":"NULL",
              "MODEL": "A1",
              "PRICE":99.99,
              "PRINT_RESOLUTION":{"RESOLUTION_H_DPI":600,
                   "RESOLUTION_V_DPI":600},
              "PRINT_SPEED_B":14,
              "PRINTING_METHOD":"LASER"}
}
```

*Fig. 7.4.  Content of the JSON file "filename.json" linked to the web page.*

## 7.4.2  Real-Time Internet Search

As already mentioned, the keyword search is not designed to be real time. Processing web pages and updating indexes may take significant time. It could be days or weeks before the updated web pages would appear in search results. Information can become stale or completely disappear during this period. In Section 7.4.1, we discussed the structured Internet search technology based on key-object instances embedded or linked to the web pages, subsequently collected by the web crawlers and loaded into data stores, and thus made searchable. This structured search is not real time as well because it relies on the web crawlers just like the keyword-based search technology does.

However, it is not the only possibility as far as the structured search is concerned. It can be made real time for websites that would like to play an active role in search instead of the passive role the websites currently play in the traditional scenario. Particularly, the "active" websites could choose to participate in the federative network of search providers based on the key-objects they would like to subscribe to. This is the kind of federative structured search framework described in Chapter 4, where some Internet websites become the data providers.

For example, e-commerce vendors could subscribe with a search provider to support certain key-objects reflecting the merchandise they sell. Their websites would need to be able to provide web-services allowing to receive the federative KeySQL queries from search providers and return relevant instances of key-objects reflecting real-time prices and inventories for their particular types of merchandise. When the search provider receives a structured query involving a key-object, it will broadcast the query to all e-commerce vendors also known as data providers that have subscribed to this key-object. The search results from the data providers will then be combined, ordered as specified by the query, and returned to the query originator along with the optional advertisements based on the real-time analysis of the query. The real-time and nonreal-time search results can also be combined within the federative framework.

In future, the real-time structured Internet search may become as ubiquitous as the keyword search is at the time of writing.

Printed in the United States
By Bookmasters